SOUP *for* SYRIA

SOUP *for* SYRIA

Recipes to Celebrate Our
Shared Humanity

Collected and Photographed by
Barbara Abdeni Massaad

Interlink Books

An imprint of Interlink Publishing Group, Inc.
Northampton, Massachusetts

First published in 2016 by

INTERLINK BOOKS
An imprint of Interlink Publishing Group, Inc.
46 Crosby Street, Northampton, Massachusetts 01060
www.interlinkbooks.com

Library of Congress Cataloging-in-Publication Data
Massaad, Barbara Abdeni.
Soup for Syria : recipes to celebrate our shared humanity /
collected and photographed by Barbara Abdeni Massaad.
    pages cm
Includes index.
ISBN 978-1-56656-089-4
1. Soups. 2. International cooking. 3. Food relief—Syria. 4. Peace-building—Syria. I. Title.
TX757.M38 2015
641.81'3--dc23   2015017058

General editor: Michel S. Moushabeck
Senior editor: Leyla Moushabeck
Copyeditor: Jennifer M. Staltare
Production: Pam Fontes-May
Book design: Pascale Hares
Photo editing: 53dots.com

Printed and bound in China
10 9 8 7 6 5 4 3 2 1

To request our complete 48-page, full-color catalog, please call us toll free at 1-800-238-LINK,
visit our website at www.interlinkbooks.com, or send us an e-mail: info@interlinkbooks.com.

Slow Food®
Beirut

Also by Barbara Abdeni Massaad

Man'oushé: Inside the Lebanese Street Corner Bakery
Mouneh: Preserving Foods for the Lebanese Pantry
Mezze: A Labor of Love

"When I visited the Syrian refugees in Lebanon, I said to them: 'Had I been a barber, I would have cut your hair for free. Because I am a cookbook author and photographer, I am doing what I can do to help through my work.'"

—Barbara Abdeni Massaad

"*Soup for Syria* may be the most compelling cookbook ever created. Through her photographs and collected recipes, Barbara Massaad directly connects us with a people in dire need of our help. Just holding this book is nourishment for the soul."

—Jim Clancy, former CNN Correspondent and Anchor, awarded A.H. Boerma medal for coverage of food and hunger issues by the UN's F.A.O.

"Soup is the ultimate comfort food; war is not. *Soup for Syria* gently stirs the two together: a variety of comfort-ready recipes from well-known food writers and chefs share the pages with a variety of faces—often smiling, always with eyes wide open—of the Syrian refugee crisis. The intimate photographs are a gentle reminder of the discomforts beyond our kitchen; the recipes the opportunity to experiment with a global collection of soup ideas... As we indulge in these recipes, we pray for the day Syrians will once again be able to sit down together over a bowl of soup in their own kitchens."

—Alia Yunis, filmmaker and author of *The Night Counter*

"You give but little when you give of your possessions. It is when you give of yourself that you truly give."

—Kahlil Gibran, from *The Prophet*

Table of Contents

Foreword

It is an honor for me to endorse the *Soup for Syria* book project.

The moment I heard about *Soup for Syria* I was hooked. The tragedy of the Syrian people touches us all, but the more than 3.8 million refugees cry out for concrete actions of solidarity. We are all called upon to build bridges, and this book is there to connect us with the most vulnerable.

Slow Food has always been at the forefront of trying to build bridges, which is the very essence of Terra Madre—our worldwide network uniting producers, consumers, chefs, academics, and youth to change the food system and make it good, clean, and fair.

I truly hope that through this book you will be able to organize, on the 10th of December, a Terra Madre Day in one or more of the refugee camps, reaffirming that the right to good, clean, and fair food is universal. The effort to keep our unique food traditions alive is the key to our dignity and our future, even in the midst of very harsh conditions. For we have all been migrants, compelled by hunger or war to seek a better life.

We should always remember that one day we could be the next ones in need.

Carlo Petrini
Slow Food founder and president

Introduction

Forty-five minutes away from my warm, cozy apartment in the Bekaa Valley is a makeshift refugee camp—one of several in Lebanon—where Syrian families crowd into plastic tents and children die of cold and hunger. I try to sleep and ignore this reality, but it's impossible. I am not immune to the suffering of others.

Refugees are people forced to leave their homes and their land to escape war or persecution, seeking security for themselves and their families. Instead of being welcomed, they are most often mistreated and misunderstood.

I am a food writer and photographer. How can I use my trade to help the unfortunate and send a message of peace through the two great passions of my life: food and photography? I started taking trips to the refugee camps, filling up the trunk of my car each time with food. After several trips, I got to know many of the families residing in the camp; they have become part of my extended family.

I spent the winter of 2014/2015 visiting them every week. The more I visited—the more of their stories I heard, and the more desperation I witnessed—the more heartbroken I became. I was determined to help no matter what. Are we not all human beings seeking the same things for our families—love, food, and shelter?

The enormity of this humanitarian crisis hit me like a ton of bricks. Why has it not galvanized a global outcry of support and aid from all corners of the world? Why has the world abandoned the Syrian refugees? And why is the humanitarian assistance from the wealthiest nations of the world facing critical shortfalls? In a recent plea, Hanaa Singer, Unicef's representative in Syria said: "We are urging longer-term investment by donors so that children can survive and start to build the next phase of their lives. We can't give up on the people of Syria."

No, we can't give up! I want to see the children survive. That is why I embarked on the *Soup for Syria* project, a humanitarian campaign to help deliver food and essential foodstuffs to the refugees. My hope is that you will join me by becoming a *Soup for Syria* goodwill ambassador. Find out how you can help by visiting www.soupforsyria. com. The funds generated from the sales of this cookbook—with photographs of Syrian refugees from the Bekaa Valley and soup recipes from highly accomplished international chefs and cookbook authors—will make a small contribution towards easing the suffering of the 3.8 million refugees.

This experience has changed my life tremendously. It has taught me what most prophets, philosophers, and people of faith try to teach their disciples. I am a better person now. And I am not alone. We are not alone! Each and every one who participated in the creation of this work has contributed to this beautiful message—a message of hope.

Stock

Beef
Stock

MAKES ABOUT 14 cups (3.5 l)

---

4 lb (2 kg) beef bones

2 onions, quartered

2 celery stalks, chopped

2 carrots, chopped

2 teaspoons black peppercorns

3–4 fresh bay leaves

Preheat the oven to 400°F (200°C). Roast the beef bones on an oven tray for 1 hour or until browned.

In a large pot, mix the bones and onions with 24 cups (6 l) of water. Add the celery, carrots, black peppercorns, and bay leaves. Bring to a boil, then simmer, uncovered, for about 3 hours, skimming the surface every so often.

Add 12 cups (3 l) of additional water and simmer, uncovered, for about 1 hour.

Strain the stock through a sieve lined with cheesecloth or muslin. Discard the solids. Allow the stock to cool, then cover and refrigerate until cold. Skim and discard the fat from the surface before use.

Chicken Stock

MAKES ABOUT 14 cups (3.5 l)

———————————————

4 lb (2 kg) chicken bones

2 onions, quartered

2 celery stalks, chopped

2 carrots, chopped

2 teaspoons black peppercorns

3 fresh bay leaves

———————————————

In a large soup pot, combine the bones, onions, and 20 cups (5 l) water. Add the celery, carrots, black peppercorns, and bay leaves. Bring to a boil, then simmer, uncovered, for about 2 hours, skimming the surface every so often.

Add 12 cups (3 l) of additional water and simmer, uncovered, for 1 hour.

Strain the stock through a sieve lined with cheesecloth or muslin. Discard the solids. Allow stock to cool, then cover and refrigerate until cold. Skim and discard the fat from the surface before use.

Fish
Stock

MAKES ABOUT 10 cups (2.5 l)

————————————

3 lb (1.5 kg) fish bones

1 onion, quartered

2 celery stalks, chopped

2 carrots, chopped

1 teaspoon black peppercorns

2 fresh bay leaves

————————————

In a large pot, mix the bones and onion with 12 cups (3 l) of water. Add the celery, carrots, black peppercorns, and bay leaves. Bring to a boil, then simmer, uncovered, for about 20 minutes, skimming the surface every so often.

Add 12 cups (3 l) of additional water and simmer, uncovered, for 1 hour.

Strain the stock through a sieve lined with cheesecloth or muslin. Discard the solids. Allow the stock to cool, then cover and refrigerate until cold. Skim and discard the fat from the surface before use.

Fish

Vegetable Stock

MAKES ABOUT 14 cups (3.5 l)

_____

4–5 onions, quartered

10 celery stalks, chopped

1 bunch parsley

2 large carrots, chopped

2 zucchinis, chopped

2 teaspoons black peppercorns

4 fresh bay leaves

_____

Combine all the ingredients in a large soup pot and add 24 cups (6 l) of water. Bring to a boil, lower the heat, and simmer, uncovered, for about 1½ hours.

Strain the stock through a sieve lined with cheesecloth or muslin and discard any solids. Allow the stock to cool, cover, and refrigerate until use.

Chris Borunda

Corn Stock

MAKES ABOUT 8 cups (2 l)

―――――――――

8 ears fresh corn, cut in half

   (or use leftover corn cobs)

¼ cup (60 ml) vegetable oil

1 large onion, chopped

2 large carrots, peeled and chopped

1 celery stalk, chopped

2 potatoes, peeled and cubed

2 fresh bay leaves

1 cinnamon stick

1 teaspoon black pepper

1 tablespoon ground coriander

1 teaspoon ground allspice

1 small bunch parsley

1 small bunch cilantro

16 cups (4 l) cold water

3 tablespoons salt

―――――――――

Hold each ear of corn vertically over a baking sheet. Use a sharp knife to slice off the kernels (you can use the kernels to make corn soup, page 81).

In a large pot, heat oil over medium heat and add the corn cobs and vegetables. Cover the pan and cook for 15 minutes, stirring occasionally.

Add the herbs and spices and cook for another 2 minutes.

Add the water and bring to a boil. Lower the heat, add the salt, and simmer for 30 minutes.

Strain the stock through a sieve lined with cheesecloth or muslin and discard the solids. Check for seasoning. If the stock tastes a little weak return it to a simmer until the volume of liquid is reduced by one third. Allow stock to cool, cover, and refrigerate until use.

Corn

Soup

Alexis Couquelet

Artichoke Soup

SERVES 4-6

---

1 lb (450 g) mushrooms

2 lb (1 kg) frozen artichoke hearts, thawed

¼–½ cup (60–120 ml) sunflower oil

½ lb (250 g) onion, chopped

½ lb (250 g) potato, peeled and cubed

8½ cups (2 l) chicken stock

1 cup (250 ml) cream

Salt and freshly ground black pepper,
    to taste

Clean the mushrooms using a brush and cut them into quarters. Halve the artichoke hearts.

Heat the oil in a large pot and sauté the onion for about 5 minutes. Add the potatoes and sauté for another 5 minutes. Add the artichoke hearts and sauté for 1 minute more.

Add the chicken stock. Bring to a boil. lower the heat. and simmer for 15 minutes.

Add the mushrooms and simmer for another 15 minutes.

Purée the soup using a blender. food processor. or immersion blender.

Return to a clean pot set over low heat. Add the cream. stir well. and taste for seasoning. Add salt and pepper as necessary. Simmer for an additional 5 minutes to heat through before serving.

Artichoke

"We at Couqley decided to participate in this noble project to show the world that despite the daily acts of cruelties in our war-torn region, there are people who care about other people. There are people who value humanity over politics, power, war, and destruction. There are people who want to help other people just because they are human and that's what humans must do."

—Alexis Couquelet

Veronica Pecorella

Green Asparagus Soup with Poached Eggs and Sautéd Shrimp

SERVES 4

---

2 lb (1 kg) green asparagus

1 medium onion, coarsely chopped

1 leek, trimmed and chopped

1 tablespoon extra virgin olive oil

Salt, to taste

Freshly ground black pepper

4 eggs

1 tablespoon butter

12 medium-size cooked shrimp, shelled

Using a vegetable peeler, peel the asparagus up to 1 inch (2 cm) from the tip, reserving the peel. Separate the stalks from the tips.

Cook the stalks in salted boiling water for at least 10 minutes, remove them with a slotted spoon, and plunge them into ice water so that they stop cooking and maintain their color.

Cook the tips in the same boiling water for only 3 minutes for a crunchy texture. Remove them with a slotted spoon and plunge them into another bowl of ice water.

Cook the skins in the boiling water for 30 minutes to make a stock. Strain the stock and let it cool.

Sauté the onion and leek in the olive oil until translucent.

Purée the stalks together with the onion and leek, adding the stock, a little at a time, until smooth and creamy.

Pour the purée into a saucepan, add the asparagus tips, heat gently, and season to taste with salt and pepper.

Poach the eggs for 30 seconds in boiling salted water and a drop of white wine vinegar.

Heat the butter in a saucepan and sauté the shrimp briefly until they color.

Transfer the asparagus purée to soup bowls and top with the poached eggs and shrimp. Serve warm.

Asparagus

Martyna Monaco

Avocado, Cucumber, and Mint Soup (chilled)

SERVES 4

---

2 avocados, peeled and cubed

4 baby cucumbers, peeled and chopped

1 small bunch parsley, roughly chopped

1 small bunch fresh mint, leaves only

1 onion, roughly chopped

Freshly squeezed juice of 2 lemons

1 cup (250 g) plain yogurt

1 cup (250 ml) cold water

Salt and white pepper, to taste

Cucumber slices, mint leaves,
    or croutons, to garnish

Combine the avocado, cucumbers, parsley, mint, onion, lemon juice, and yogurt in a blender or food processor. Blend until smooth.

Gradually add water until you reach your desired consistency.

Season with salt and white pepper.

Chill in the refrigerator for at least 30 minutes before serving.

Garnish with cucumber slices, mint leaves, or croutons, if desired.

"*Soup for Syria* is not only a book, but a huge opportunity to understand the value of human dignity. Now, more than ever before, Syrian refugees need our help."

—Martyna Monaco

Jane Hughes

Black Bean and Chipotle Chowder

SERVES 4

---

1 teaspoon vegetable oil

2 small onions, diced

3 small carrots, diced

4 celery stalks, diced

3 garlic cloves, crushed

1 jalapeño pepper, seeded and
   finely chopped

1 tablespoon unsweetened cocoa powder

1 tablespoon ground chipotle powder

1 teaspoon cumin

3 medium sweet potatoes, diced

1 lb (450 g) fresh tomatoes, diced

4¼ cups (1 l) vegetable stock

28 oz (800 g) canned or cooked black beans,
   drained and rinsed

Zest and juice of 1 lime

1 teaspoon salt, or to taste

Fresh cilantro, to garnish

Warm the oil in a large pan and gently fry the onions, carrots, and celery for 5 minutes. Stir in the garlic, jalapeño, cocoa, chipotle, and cumin and cook until fragrant, about 3 minutes.

Add the sweet potatoes, stir together well, and cook for a further 3 minutes. Add the tomatoes and stock, bring to a boil, then reduce the heat and simmer, covered, for 25 minutes or until the sweet potatoes are tender.

Add the beans, lime zest, and juice and heat through. Taste and season with salt to your liking. Garnish with cilantro.

Bean

"I find making soup very grounding—it's about turning scraps into something nourishing, and in the process taking care of yourself and others. I'm humbled by the thought that one of my soup recipes could make a difference to Syrian refugees and glad to be a part of this project."

—Jane Hughes

Claudia Roden

Borlotti Bean and Pasta Soup

SERVES 6

---

1 cup (200 g) dried borlotti beans,
    soaked overnight in cold water

3 tablespoons extra virgin olive oil,
    plus more to drizzle

¼ lb (125 g) bacon, chopped

1 celery stalk, chopped

1 onion, chopped

1 carrot, peeled and chopped

2 small garlic cloves, coarsely chopped

3 tomatoes, peeled and chopped

Salt and freshly ground black pepper,
    to taste

1 cup (100 g) uncooked penne or other
    short tubular pasta

Grated Parmesan or Grana Padano

Heat the oil in a large saucepan and sauté the bacon, celery, onion, carrot, and garlic until the vegetables have softened, stirring often.

Add the tomatoes and cook over medium heat for 10 minutes.

Drain and add the beans, cover with water, and simmer gently for 1–2 hours, or until they are tender, topping them up with water every so often. Add salt and pepper once the beans have begun to soften.

Remove a ladleful of beans, purée them in a blender, and return them to the soup.

Add the pasta and cook until it is done a bit more than al dente.

Serve with pepper and a dribble of olive oil on each serving and pass the cheese.

"My hope is that this project is a success and the book helps to keep the plight of Syrian refugees in people's minds and that it will raise funds to alleviate their awful living conditions until their future is settled. *Pasta e fasioi* (Venetian dialect for 'beans') is an old peasant dish in the Veneto. The soup varies from one city to another—wide tagliatelle are used in Vicenza, whole wheat noodles called bigoli in Verona, lasagne in Este and Padua, and thin fettuccine or small tubular pasta in other parts. I am so glad that it is part of this humanitarian project."

—Claudia Roden

Bean

Greg Malouf

Persian Bean Soup

SERVES 6-8

_____

¼ cup (60 ml) extra virgin olive oil

2 medium onions, finely chopped

½ teaspoon turmeric

½ teaspoon ground black pepper

2 teaspoons ground cumin

10½ cups (2.5 l) vegetable stock

¼ cup (50 g) dried red kidney beans,
    soaked overnight and drained

¼ cup (50 g) dried navy beans,
    soaked overnight and drained

¼ cup (50 g) dried chickpeas,
    soaked overnight and drained

½ cup (100 g) French lentils

2 teaspoons sea salt

Small bunch chives, chopped

Small bunch dill, chopped

Small bunch parsley, coarsely chopped

2 cups (60 g) spinach, chopped

1 cup (40 g) coarsely chopped
    Swiss chard leaves

½ cup (120 ml) sour cream

_____

Heat the olive oil in a large soup pot over medium heat and sauté onions and spices.

Pour in the vegetable stock. Add the kidney beans, navy beans, and chickpeas. Bring to a boil, lower the heat to simmer, and cover the pot. Simmer for 45 minutes, or until the beans are just cooked. Add the lentils and more stock, if needed. Cook for an additional 30 minutes or until the lentils are tender.

Add the salt, chives, dill, parsley, spinach, and Swiss chard leaves. Cook for a further 5 minutes, stirring occasionally. Check the seasoning and add more stock if the soup is too thick.

Stir in the sour cream, setting aside a heaped tablespoon for garnish. Bring the soup back to a boil then serve, topped with a dollop of sour cream.

"I've always believed that there is no better way to banish differences and bring people together than through sharing food. And soup is, perhaps, the ultimate shared dish. It's a small enough thing, to contribute a recipe, but perhaps the many small voices that have joined together in this lovely book can, together, sing a loud message of hope."

—Greg Malouf

Bean

Anthony Bourdain

Soupe au Pistou

SERVES 6

---

1 cup (225 g) dried white beans (pinto, great
    northern, or Tarbais are all good), soaked

2 tablespoons olive oil

2 garlic cloves, thinly sliced—as in Goodfellas

1 medium onion, diced small

1 lb (450 g) seeded, chopped, fresh, ripe tomatoes

2 leeks, washed thoroughly and cut into
    ¼ inch (6 mm) slices

2 small zucchinis, diced small (Remember to use
    only the outer parts of the zucchini and the
    yellow squash: do not use the seed cavities.
    Throw them out.)

2 small yellow squash, diced small

1 fennel bulb, diced small

4 cups (900 ml) light chicken stock or broth

1 bouquet garni

3 oz (75 g) elbow macaroni

Salt and pepper

PISTOU

1 bunch fresh basil leaves, picked from stems,
    washed, and dried

6 garlic cloves

½ cup (120 ml) extra virgin olive oil

4 oz (112 g) grated Parmesan cheese

Salt and pepper

First: The day before you make the soup, soak the beans in plenty of cold water for 24 hours. (Since you have time, you might consider making your own chicken stock at this point.)

The next day, put on some music. Drain and rinse the beans, then cook in either water or chicken stock until nearly done—meaning still a little hard in the middle. Do not cook the beans to mush, please. When ready, drain and rinse in cold water to arrest cooking. Put aside. You'll need them later. Do all your knife work, meaning the dicing, slicing, and so on.

Now we are ready to begin the actual cooking. Right? You've got everything? Assemble your prepped ingredients in an organized fashion. You've got your 'meez' together? Let's go...

In a large, heavy-bottomed pot, heat the olive oil. When the oil is hot, add the garlic and onion and sauté on low heat for a few moments to release the flavors. When the onion begins to clear and become translucent, add the rest of the vegetables and continue to sauté on low heat (sweating them) until slightly soft. Add the chicken stock or broth and the bouquet garni and bring to a quick boil on high heat, then immediately reduce the heat until you have a nice, gentle simmer. Add the elbow macaroni and continue simmering until it's nearly cooked through. Drop in the beans. Simmer, stirring occasionally, remembering to skim, skim, skim with a ladle to remove scum and foam.

While the soup is simmering, make the pistou. In a mortar and pestle, grind and pound the basil and garlic together until it becomes a sludgelike paste. With a fork, slowly incorporate the olive oil a little at a time. Fold in the Parmesan at the end. Season with salt and pepper. You can, I suppose, cheat and use a food processor for this; plenty of, if not most, restaurants probably do. But that would be wrong.

After about 30 minutes, when the soup is ready (meaning the macaroni and the beans are cooked through but not mushy or overcooked, still maintaining their structural integrity), whisk in your pistou, salt and pepper to taste, and serve immediately.

Most soups get better the next day. This is not one of them. Anytime you've got pasta, zucchini, or squash incorporated in a soup, it's going to get ugly the next day. Ditto basil paste. This lovely, colorful, fresh-tasting soup will turn a nasty, army fatigue color by tomorrow. And the pistou will take over the soup. So eat it all now.

"Soup is elemental, and it always makes sense, even when the world around us fails to."

—Anthony Bourdain

Patrick Herbeaux

Red Beet Gazpacho (chilled)

SERVES 6

_____

1 lb (450 g) red beets, cooked and peeled

½ lb (250 g) tomatoes, roughly chopped

¼ (50 g) of a red or orange bell pepper,
  roughly chopped

4 oz (100 g) toasted bread, cubed

½ cup (50 g) roasted pistachios

3 tablespoons cider vinegar

½ cup (120 ml) extra virgin olive oil

Salt, to taste

Croutons, to garnish (optional)

_____

Combine the beets, tomatoes, bell peppers, bread, pistachios, vinegar, and olive oil in a blender or food processor. Blend to get a smooth consistency.

Add salt to taste. Chill for at least 30 minutes before serving.

Serve with croutons, if desired.

"It was only natural for me to participate and give a helping hand in this project. I wanted to share and live this different human experience. And it was a great one made possible by the lovely people I met— especially those refugees for whom this book project is intended."

—Patrick Herbeaux

Beet

Barbara Abdeni Massaad

Roasted
Red Beet
Soup

SERVES 4-6

1 lb (450 g) red beets

1 tablespoon butter

1 tablespoon extra virgin olive oil

2 leeks, trimmed and chopped

1 medium onion, sliced

2 celery stalks, chopped

¼ teaspoon ground ginger

¼ teaspoon ground allspice

¼ teaspoon white pepper

1 bay leaf

1 fresh thyme sprig

2 fresh parsley sprigs

½ cup (120 ml) cream,

    plus ¼ cup (60 ml) for garnish (optional)

Salt and freshly ground black

    pepper, to taste

Preheat the oven to 400°F (200°C). Wrap the beets in foil and roast until tender when pierced with a fork, about 1 hour.

Cool the beets and peel. Cut half of 1 beet into small cubes and set aside for the garnish. Chop the remaining beets into ½ inch (1 cm) pieces.

Melt the butter with the oil in a heavy medium-size saucepan over medium-high heat. Add the leek, onion, and celery and cook until they begin to brown, stirring frequently. This should take about 15 minutes.

Stir in ginger, allspice, white pepper, and beets. Cook, stirring, until the vegetables begin to stick to the bottom of the pot, about 5 minutes.

Add 4¼ cups (1 l) water, the bay leaf, thyme, and parsley. Bring to a boil. Reduce heat to low, cover, and simmer until the vegetables are very tender, about 25 minutes. Remove the bay leaf, thyme, and parsley.

To purée the soup, fill a blender or food processor no more than halfway. Start on low speed, keeping your hand on top in case the lid pops off from the rising steam. Increase the speed to high and blend until smooth, about 1 minute. You might need to do this in batches.

Return the soup to a clean pot set over low heat. Add the cream and salt and pepper to taste. Stir well.

Ladle into soup bowls. Garnish each serving with the reserved beet cubes and 1 tablespoon of cream, if desired.

Martyna Monaco

Broccoli and Leek Soup

SERVES 4

---

1 cup (250 ml) whole milk

2 tablespoons (30 g) butter

3 tablespoons flour

Salt, to taste

Freshly ground black pepper, to taste

Freshly ground nutmeg, to taste

2 tablespoons extra virgin olive oil

4 leeks, trimmed and chopped

1 large head of broccoli, broken into florets

4¼ cups (1 l) vegetable stock

Heat the milk in a saucepan over low heat for 5 minutes.

In another saucepan, melt the butter over low heat and add the flour, stirring well until smooth. Add the milk and stir quickly until you have a smooth white sauce. Add salt, black pepper, and nutmeg to taste. Remove from the heat and set aside.

Heat the oil in a soup pot over medium-high heat. Add the chopped leek and sauté until golden brown. Add the broccoli and the stock, stir well, and bring to a simmer. Cook over medium heat until the broccoli is soft and the broth has reduced by half.

To purée the soup, fill a blender or food processor no more than halfway. Start on low speed, keeping your hand on top in case the lid pops off from the rising steam. Increase the speed to high and blend until smooth, about 1 minute. You might need to do this in batches.

Return to a clean pot set over low heat. Add the white sauce, stir well, and taste for seasoning. Return to the heat for 5 minutes to heat through.

Broccoli

Aline Kamakian and
Serge Maacaron

Armenian Cabbage Soup

SERVES 6-8

_____

2 tablespoons extra virgin olive oil

1 onion, finely chopped

1 small green cabbage, thinly sliced

3 small potatoes, cubed

2 medium zucchinis, sliced (optional)

1 cup (150 g) coarse bulgar (*burghul*)

2 cups (500 g) yogurt

Dried ground mint (optional)

Salt, to taste

_____

In a medium soup pot, heat the olive oil over medium-high heat. Sauté the onion, stirring frequently, for 2-3 minutes. Add the cabbage, potatoes, and zucchini and mix.

Add the bulgar and cook, stirring constantly, until the cabbage starts to soften.

Add 4¼ cups (1 l) water and bring to a boil. Lower the heat and simmer for 5 minutes.

Add the yogurt to the hot soup and mix until the yogurt is completely diluted in the broth.

Add the dried mint, if using, and salt.

Serve warm or at room temperature.

Sona Tikidjian

Spicy Cabbage Soup

SERVES 4-6

½ cup (120 ml) extra virgin olive oil

1 large onion, chopped

3 tablespoons tomato paste

1–2 teaspoons red pepper paste (medium/hot)

1 medium green cabbage, sliced

1 cup (150 g) fine bulgar (*burghul*)

Juice of 1 lemon

Salt, to taste

Heat the olive oil in a large saucepan or soup pot and sauté the onion. Add the tomato and red pepper pastes and mix well.

Add the cabbage and bulgar. Cook for 5 minutes.

Add 4¼ cups (1 l) water. Bring to a boil, lower the heat, and simmer for about 20 minutes, uncovered, until the cabbage is tender.

Season with lemon juice and salt. Serve warm.

Cabbage

Zeina El Zein Maktabi

Carrot and Ginger Soup

SERVES 4-6

———————————

3 tablespoons (40 g) butter

1 onion, finely chopped

6–7 large carrots, peeled and sliced

1 potato, peeled and cubed

Salt, to taste

2 cups (475 ml) chicken or
   vegetable stock

Zest of 1 orange

1 tablespoon grated ginger

Ginger shavings, to garnish

———————————

Melt the butter in a large soup pot over medium heat. Add the onion. Cook and stir for about 3 minutes until soft but not brown.

Stir in the carrots and potato. Cook for 5–6 minutes, stirring frequently. Sprinkle with salt.

Add the chicken or vegetable stock and 2 cups (475 ml) water. Bring to a boil. Add the orange zest and ginger. Lower the heat, cover the pan, and simmer, stirring occasionally, until the vegetables are tender, about 30-35 minutes.

To purée the soup, fill a blender or food processor no more than halfway. Start on low speed, keeping your hand on top in case the lid pops off from the rising steam. Increase the speed to high and blend until smooth, about 1 minute. You might need to do this in batches.

Serve the soup warm, garnished with ginger shavings.

Carrot

Alice Waters

Carrot Soup

SERVES 8

———————————

4 tablespoons (60 g) butter

2 onions, sliced

1 sprig thyme

2½ lb (1 kg) carrots, peeled and sliced

2 teaspoons salt, or to taste

6 cups (1.5 l) chicken or vegetable stock

½ cup (120 ml) whipped cream or
    crème fraîche (optional)

Freshly ground black pepper, to taste

Small handful chervil, chives, or tarragon,
    finely chopped (optional)

A spoonful of cumin seeds (optional)

———————————

Melt the butter in a heavy-bottomed pot over medium-low heat. Add the onions and thyme. Cook, stirring occasionally, until the onions are tender, about 10 minutes.

Add the carrots, season with salt, and cook for 5 minutes. (Cooking the carrots with the onions for a while concentrates the flavor.)

Add the stock and bring to a boil. Lower the heat and simmer until the carrots are tender, about 30 minutes.

When done, season with salt to taste and purée, if desired.

Serve the soup warm. Garnish with a bit of whipped cream or crème fraîche seasoned with salt and pepper and chopped chervil, chives, or tarragon.

Alternatively, heat some butter or olive oil, sizzle a spoonful of cumin seeds in it, and spoon this over the soup as a garnish instead.

"Whether we are in times of crisis or times of peace, gathering family and friends together around the table and sharing food is one of the most powerful and life-affirming acts we can do. And there is nothing more comforting and nourishing than a bowl of warm soup."

—Alice Waters

Linda Toubia

Cauliflower Soup

SERVES 4

_____

1 medium cauliflower

2 tablespoons extra virgin olive oil

1 medium onion, finely chopped

1 garlic clove, finely chopped

1 small bunch cilantro, finely chopped

1 tablespoon tomato paste

4 large tomatoes, peeled and chopped

1 teaspoon red pepper paste

Salt, to taste

Freshly ground black pepper, to taste

½ cup (100 g) short-grain rice

_____

Fill a large stockpot with water and bring to a boil.

Rinse the cauliflower under cold water. Cut away the outer leaves, core the cauliflower, and cut into large florets. Blanch the florets in the boiling water for about 3 minutes, ensuring that the water remains at a full boil. Prepare a large bowl of ice water while the cauliflower blanches.

Carefully drain the cauliflower florets and transfer to the ice bath. Allow the florets to rest in the ice bath for 1–2 minutes, then drain thoroughly.

Heat the oil in a soup pot over medium-high heat. Add the onion, garlic, and cilantro. Sauté for 2-3 minutes, stirring occasionally.

Dilute the tomato paste in 4¼ cups (1 l) water and add it to the pot, along with the blanched cauliflower, tomatoes, red pepper paste, salt, and pepper. Bring to a boil and lower the heat to simmer.

Add the rice, partially cover the pot, and simmer gently until rice is cooked, about 20-30 minutes, checking from time to time.

Serve warm in soup bowls.

"_Soup for Syria_ is a wonderful initiative that will gather people around the world over a bowl of soup and a desire to help."

—Linda Toubia

Sana Wakeem Awad

Curried Cauliflower Soup

SERVES 4-6

---

2 tablespoons vegetable oil

1 onion, chopped

4 small garlic cloves, chopped

1 medium cauliflower, broken into florets

½ teaspoon freshly ground black pepper

1 teaspoon curry powder

1 teaspoon grated fresh ginger

   (or substitute ½ teaspoon ground ginger)

½ teaspoon turmeric

½ teaspoon cumin

Salt, to taste

4¼ cups (1 l) chicken or vegetable stock

1 bunch scallions, finely chopped

Heat the oil in a large soup pot over medium-high heat. Add the onion and garlic and sauté for 2-3 minutes, stirring occasionally.

Add the cauliflower and cook for another 1–2 minutes, then add the spices and salt. Stir well and cook for 2 minutes.

Add the stock, stir well, and bring to a simmer. Cook over medium heat until cauliflower is tender.

To purée the soup, fill a blender or food processor no more than halfway. Start on a low speed, keeping your hand on top in case the lid pops off from the rising steam. Increase the speed to high and blend until smooth, about 1 minute. You might need to do this in batches.

Serve hot in soup bowls, garnished with the chopped scallions.

"I am touched and moved by this noble mission. I wish you strength and hope *Soup for Syria* will be a success and help those refugees in need. Well done!"

—Sana Wakeem Awad

Cauliflower

Helena Zakharia

Chicken Soup

SERVES 6-8

_____

3 chicken legs, fat removed

1 large onion, roughly chopped

½ teaspoon cinnamon

½ teaspoon allspice

Salt, to taste

2 zucchinis, finely chopped

2 carrots, finely chopped

1 tomato, finely chopped

4–5 tablespoons broken vermicelli

Juice of 1–2 lemons

1 small bunch parsley,
    roughly chopped

_____

Place the chicken in a large pot with 8 cups (2 l) water. Bring to a boil over medium-high heat, skimming off any foam that rises to the surface. Reduce the heat to simmer, and add the onion, cinnamon, allspice, and salt. Simmer gently until chicken is cooked, about 45 minutes. Continue to skim off the foam occasionally.

Lift the chicken from the broth and set aside to cool. Remove the bone, cartilage, and skin from the chicken and discard. Separate the meat into small pieces.

Add the chopped vegetables to the broth and cook until tender, about 25 minutes. Add the chicken pieces, vermicelli, and lemon juice. Adjust the seasoning and simmer for a few more minutes until the vermicelli is cooked al dente.

Serve steaming hot and topped with a sprinkle of chopped parsley.

"It was a wonderful opportunity for me to be part of this amazing project. I enjoyed sharing my family's soup recipes. What a blessing it was for me and my daughter, Maya, to be able to participate in such a worthy cause and to meet such amazing people."

—Helena Zakharia

Yotam Ottolenghi and Sami Tamimi

Gondi

SERVES 4

---

1 tablespoon olive oil

4 chicken thighs (1¼ lb/600 g), bone in and skin on

2 medium onions, peeled and quartered

1 large carrot, peeled and cut into 1 inch (3 cm) chunks

½ teaspoon ground turmeric

2 whole Iranian dried limes, pierced with a
   knife a couple of times

Small handful (30 g) parsley, tied into a bunch

20 whole black peppercorns

1 teaspoon salt

9 oz (250 g) cooked cannellini beans (canned are fine)

About 1 tablespoon lime juice, to serve

About ½ cup (10 g) picked cilantro leaves, to serve

DUMPLINGS

9 oz (250 g) ground chicken (or Turkey if unavailable)

1½ tablespoons (25 g) melted unsalted butter

1 cup (100 g) chickpea (gram) flour

1 medium onion, finely chopped in a food
   processor (6 oz/180 g net)

½ cup (10 g) parsley, finely chopped

½ teaspoon ground cardamom

½ teaspoon ground cumin

¼ teaspoon ground turmeric

1 tablespoon rosewater

¼ teaspoon crushed black peppercorns

1 teaspoon salt

Heat the oil in a medium stockpot on medium heat. Add the chicken thighs and sauté lightly for 8 minutes, turning once. Add the onions, carrot, turmeric, dried limes, parsley, peppercorns, and salt. Pour over 6 cups (1.5 l) water, bring to a gentle simmer, cover, and cook for 40 minutes. Use a slotted spoon to remove all the chicken and vegetables from the pan (keep the chicken to make a salad or a sandwich filling). Return the limes to the liquid and set aside.

Place all the dumpling ingredients in a mixing bowl. Mix well and, with wet hands, shape the mixture into 16 round dumplings weighing between 1 and 1½ oz (30 and 35 g) each.

Bring the broth to a gentle boil and add the cannellini beans. Carefully lower the dumplings into the broth, cover with a lid, and simmer on low heat for 30 minutes. The dumplings will expand in the liquid. Remove the lid and simmer for another 20 minutes, until a concentrated soup consistency and flavor is reached. Add more water, or reduce the liquid for longer, if necessary. Serve the soup with a drizzle of lime juice and the picked cilantro.

"Soup is the ultimate comfort food: nurturing, sustaining, and all good things. One recipe is a drop in the ocean but, if awareness of the plight of the Syrian refugees is raised with each batch made and shared, then that is a force for good. As well as being a delicious meal in and of itself."

—Yotam Ottolenghi and Sami Tamimi

Chicken

Nur Ilkin and Sheilah Kaufman

Turkish Chicken and Rice Soup

SERVES 4–6

Chicken

2 whole chicken legs (1½ lb/650 g)

1 onion, halved

1 small carrot, peeled and halved

A few sprigs flat-leaf parsley,
    tied together

1 bay leaf

6 black peppercorns

Sea salt, to taste

½ cup (100 g) medium-grain rice

2 tablespoons canola oil

1 tablespoon (15 g) butter

1 teaspoon tomato paste

1 teaspoon red pepper paste

1 tablespoon flour

1 teaspoon dried mint

½ cup (75 g) drained canned or cooked
    chickpeas

Lemon wedges, to garnish

In a large pot, bring 5 cups (1.2 l) water to a boil. Add the chicken, onion, carrot, parsley, bay leaf, peppercorns, and salt to taste. Reduce the heat, cover, and simmer until the chicken is tender, 40–45 minutes. Transfer the chicken to a plate and let it cool. Strain and reserve the cooking liquid. Once the chicken has cooled, remove the skin and bones and shred into bite-size pieces. Set aside.

In a medium–large pot, bring 1 cup (250 ml) water to a boil. Add the rice, cover, and simmer until the rice is cooked, 10–12 minutes (or follow package instructions). Add 4 cups (900 ml) of the reserved chicken stock (if there is not enough, add water) and the shredded chicken. Cook for an additional 4–5 minutes.

Meanwhile, heat the oil and butter in a small skillet. Stir in the tomato and red pepper pastes, flour, and dried mint. Mix well and pour over the soup, stiring it in well. Add the chickpeas and cook for another 5 minutes. Serve hot with lemon wedges.

"Since Turkey is a direct neighbor of Syria, and host to more than 1.5 million Syrian refugees, we witness this tragedy on a daily basis. This project that could help alleviate their suffering is most useful and timely. What is more, soup dishes are enjoyed by everyone in our part of the world. As we say in Turkey, a bowl of hot soup offered goes a long way in the minds and hearts of people."

—Nur Ilkin

Laurie Constantino

Greek Chickpea Soup with Lemon and Rosemary

SERVES 4

¼ cup (60 ml) extra virgin olive oil,
    plus more for drizzling

2 onions, diced

1 teaspoon salt, or to taste

Freshly ground black pepper, to taste

2½ cups (350 g) canned or cooked
    chickpeas, peeled if time permits

1 tablespoon plus 1 teaspoon finely chopped
    rosemary, or more to taste

¼ cup (60 ml) freshly squeezed lemon juice,
    or to taste

Rosemary sprigs, to garnish

Heat the oil in a large soup pot over medium heat. Sauté the onions, lightly seasoned with salt and pepper, until they soften and start to brown.

Stir in the chickpeas, 4¼ cups (1 l) water, and 1 tablespoon of chopped rosemary. Bring to a boil, turn down the heat, and simmer for 30-40 minutes.

Purée soup until smooth using a stick blender, food processor, or blender.

Stir in the lemon juice, salt, and 1 teaspoon of rosemary. Taste and add more salt, lemon juice, or rosemary, as needed. If soup is too thick, add more water until the texture is to your liking.

Ladle into bowls, drizzle with olive oil, and garnish with rosemary sprigs.

"Millions of Syrians have lost their homes; entire families are starving; and winter's cold cuts deep. Food relief from compassionate people around the world stands between death and the displaced."

—Laurie Constantino

Marina Ana Santos

Portuguese Chickpea Soup

SERVES 2-3

---

2 tablespoons extra virgin olive oil

1 small onion, finely chopped

2 small garlic cloves, chopped

2 carrots, peeled and chopped

1 potato, peeled and cubed

1 cup (150 g) cooked or canned chickpeas

1 lb (450 g) spinach leaves, coarsely chopped

Salt and freshly ground black pepper,
    to taste

Heat the oil in a large soup pot over medium-high heat. Add the onion and sauté for 2-3 minutes, stirring occasionally. Stir in the garlic, then add the carrots and potatoes and cook for an additonal 1-2 minutes. Add half of the chickpeas.

Add water to cover, stir well, and bring to a simmer. Partially cover the pot and cook over medium heat until vegetables are tender, about 15 minutes.

Purée the soup in a blender or food processor until smooth, about 1 minute. You might need to do this in batches.

Return to a clean pot set over low heat. Add the rest of the chickpeas and the spinach leaves and simmer for 5 minutes. Add salt and black pepper to taste.

Chris Borunda

Corn Soup

SERVES 4-6

––––––––––––

3 tablespoons extra virgin olive oil

2 large onions, diced

1 bunch scallions, thinly sliced

2 small garlic cloves, minced

2 tablespoons *baharat* spice mix

   (or use allspice)

1 tablespoon salt, or to taste

8½ cups (2 l) corn stock (see page 27)

Corn kernels reserved from stock

   (about 6 cups/1 kg)

1 small bunch parsley,

   finely chopped (optional)

1 small bunch cilantro,

   finely chopped (optional)

Lemon wedges (optional)

––––––––––––

Heat the oil in a large soup pot over medium heat. Add the onion, scallions, and garlic. Cover the pan and allow to sweat for 5 minutes.

Add the spices, salt, and corn kernels. Cover and sweat for an additional 5 minutes, checking the heat to make sure nothing browns.

Add the stock and bring to a simmer. Cook for 10 minutes. Adjust seasoning as needed.

Ladle in soup bowls and garnish with parsley, cilantro, or a squeeze of lemon. Serve hot or at room temperature.

"When I looked at the faces of those displaced children, all I could think of and see is the face of my own daughter. I immediately knew I had to help. If one child is helped because of this book and this recipe, then I have done my job as a chef, father, and human being."

—Chris Borunda

Sana Wakeem Awad

Fennel
Soup

SERVES 4

_____

2 teaspoons vegetable oil or butter

1 medium onion, chopped

2 medium fennel bulbs, thinly sliced
    (reserve the leaves)

1–2 small garlic cloves, chopped

2 carrots, peeled and julienned

6 cups (1.5 l) vegetable stock

Salt, to taste

Pinch white pepper

½ cup chopped fennel leaves

_____

Heat the oil or butter in a large soup pot over medium-high heat. Add the chopped onion and fennel and sauté for 2-3 minutes, stirring occasionally.

Add the garlic and cook for another 2 minutes. Stir in the carrots.

Add the stock, stir well, and bring to a simmer. Cook over medium heat until vegetables are soft, about 10-15 minutes.

Add salt and pepper to taste. Add the fennel leaves and simmer for 5 minutes.

Ladle the soup into bowls and serve hot.

Greg Malouf

Fennel Soup with Lemon and Cinnamon

SERVES 6-8

————————

¼ cup (60 ml) extra virgin olive oil,
   plus more to drizzle

2 onions, sliced

2 small garlic cloves, roughly chopped

2 leeks, roughly chopped

3 large fennel bulbs, sliced

2 potatoes, peeled and cut into chunks

6 cups (1.5 l) chicken stock

1 cinnamon stick

Peel of ½ a lemon

½ teaspoon allspice

2 bay leaves

Salt and freshly ground black pepper,
   to taste

2 egg yolks

½ cup (120 ml) heavy cream

Juice of 2 lemons

1 teaspoon ground cinnamon

3 tablespoons roughly chopped parsley

————————

Heat the oil in a large heavy-based saucepan and sauté the onions, garlic, leeks, and fennel for a few minutes until they soften.

Add the potatoes and chicken stock, then the cinnamon stick, lemon peel, allspice, and bay leaves. Bring to a boil, then lower the heat and gently simmer for 20 minutes. Remove and discard the cinnamon stick, lemon peel, and bay leaves, and season to taste with salt and pepper.

In a separate bowl, whisk the egg yolks with the cream, then stir in a large spoonful of the hot soup. Whisk together well, then tip the egg mixture into the soup. Slowly return the soup to just below boiling, stirring it all the time. Remove from the heat and adjust the seasoning, adding more salt and pepper and the lemon juice.

As you serve, drizzle each bowl with extra virgin olive oil and sprinkle with cinnamon and parsley.

Beatrice Khater

Spanish Garlic Soup

SERVES 4

———————

3 tablespoons extra virgin olive oil

10 small garlic cloves, thinly sliced

4 day-old slices thick rustic bread,
   coarsely chopped

2 cups (475 ml) chicken stock

Salt, to taste

4 eggs (optional)

Pinch paprika

———————

Heat the oil in a heavy soup pot over medium heat. Sauté the garlic until just golden brown, being careful not to let it burn. Stir in the bread and cook for 1 minute, allowing flavor of the garlic to seep into the bread.

Add stock and bring slowly to a boil. Reduce heat to low, cover, and simmer for 20 minutes. Add salt, if needed.

If using, crack the eggs into the soup one at a time. Allow the eggs to poach whole for 3–4 minutes.

Ladle the soup into warm bowls, making sure there is an egg in each bowl. Sprinkle with paprika and serve hot.

"It is a cold winter and the pleasure of the day is to arrive home after a long day of work and have a hot, very hot soup to drink. The warmth, the taste, and the affection you feel in each spoon are your rewards. Then images of refugees strike your head. You have sent clothes, blankets, and money to help those in need, those living under tents, freezing their bones during the long winter nights. You feel ashamed of your comfort when you know that a few kilometers away kids are dying from the cold."

—Beatrice Khater

Pascale Hares

Jerusalem Artichoke Soup

SERVES 4

————————

2 tablespoons extra virgin olive oil

1 medium onion, chopped

1 lb (450 g) Jerusalem artichokes (sunchokes),
   peeled and cubed

1 medium sweet potato, peeled and cubed

3 cups (750 ml) chicken stock

1 leek, trimmed and chopped

Zest and juice of 1 lemon

1 sprig fresh thyme

1 bay leaf, plus more to garnish

½ cup (120 ml) cream

Salt, ground black pepper, and grated
   nutmeg, to taste

————————

Heat the oil in a heavy soup pot over medium-high heat and sauté the onion for 1-2 minutes. Add the Jerusalem artichokes and sweet potato and cook for 3 minutes.

Add the stock, leek, lemon zest, thyme, and bay leaf. Bring to a boil. Reduce the heat to low, cover, and simmer until the vegetables are very tender, about 30 minutes.

Remove the bay leaf and thyme.

Purée the soup to a smooth consistency in a blender or food processor. You might need to do this in batches.

Return to a clean pot set over low heat. Add the lemon juice and cream, stirring to combine. Season with salt, pepper, and grated nutmeg and serve hot, garnished with fresh bay leaves, if desired.

"Having lived through wartime as a child, I feel a need to help the people freezing in tents, far from home, and with nothing to go back to. If you are neutral in situations of injustice, then you have chosen the side of the oppressor."

—Pascale Hares

Jerusalem Artichoke

Alexis Couquelet

Leek and Carrot Soup

SERVES 4-6

_____

3 tablespoons vegetable oil

1 large onion, finely chopped

2 lb (1 kg) leeks, trimmed and chopped

½ lb (250 g) carrots, peeled and chopped

1 lb (450 g) potatoes, peeled and cubed

8½ cups (2 l) chicken stock

1 cup (250 ml) cream

Salt and freshly ground black pepper,
    to taste

_____

Heat the oil in a large soup pot over medium-high heat. Add the chopped onion and sauté for 2-3 minutes, stirring occasionally. Add the leeks, carrots, and potatoes and cook for an additional 5 minutes.

Add the stock, stir well, and bring to a simmer. Cook over medium heat until potatoes are soft, about 30 minutes.

Purée the soup in a blender or food processor. You might need to do this in batches.

Return to a clean pot set over low heat. Slowly stir in the cream. Season with salt and pepper and serve hot.

Leek

Sana Wakeem Awad

Leek and Potato Soup

SERVES 4

_____

2 tablespoons extra virgin olive oil

1 medium onion, chopped

4–5 leeks, trimmed and chopped

1 lb (450 g) potatoes, peeled and cubed

2 small garlic cloves, finely chopped

1 bay leaf

8½ cups (2 l) chicken stock

1 cup (250 ml) milk

1 cup (250 ml) cream

Salt, to taste

Pinch white pepper

_____

Heat the oil in a large soup pot over medium-high heat. Add the chopped onion and sauté for 2-3 minutes, stirring occasionally. Add the leeks and potatoes and cook another 1–2 minutes, then add the garlic and bay leaf. Stir well and cook for 2 minutes.

Add the stock, stir well, and bring to a simmer. Cook over medium heat until the potatoes are soft, about 25 minutes. Add the milk and cook for another 5 minutes to heat through.

To purée the soup, fill a blender or food processor no more than halfway. Start on low speed, keeping your hand on top in case the lid pops off from the rising steam. Increase the speed to high and blend until smooth, about 1 minute. You might need to do this in batches.

Return to a clean pot set over low heat. Slowly stir in the cream. Add salt and pepper to taste.

Leek

Aziz Hallaj

Aleppo Red Lentil Soup with Verjuice

SERVES 4-6

---

2 cups (400 g) split red lentils

2 teaspoons Lebanese seven spice
   (or use *garam masala*)

2 teaspoons cumin

Salt, to taste

1 cup (250 ml) verjuice
   (sour grape juice; or substitute lemon juice)

1 cup (250 ml) extra virgin olive oil

10 small garlic cloves, crushed

Toasted croutons (optional)

1 teaspoon Aleppo pepper or paprika

Cover the lentils with 6 cups (1.5 l) water in a large soup pot and bring to a boil. Boil for about 30 minutes or until the lentils are very tender, skimming off any foam that forms on top.

Add the spice mix, cumin, salt, and verjuice, and cook for an additional 10 minutes or so. When done, the lentils should have broken down somewhat and thickened the soup.

In a separate pan, heat the olive oil and sauté the garlic cloves until golden brown (but not black). Pour immediately into the soup, mix well, and cook for another 2 minutes.

Garnish with croutons, if using, and a sprinkle of Aleppo pepper or paprika. Serve hot.

"Every day, about 450 people die from disease, hunger, and cold. These are not only victims in besieged areas; they are to be found in central cities and in every town and village. Poverty has now overtaken two-thirds of the Syrian people and more than half of Syrian children are out of schools. It is time to drop our vanities and recognize that we need to find solutions."

—Aziz Hallaj

Pascale Hares

Indian Lentil Soup

SERVES 4-6

---

1 tablespoon (15 g) butter

1 medium onion, chopped

1 carrot, peeled and chopped

3 small garlic cloves, finely chopped

2 tablespoons grated fresh ginger

2 small tart apples, peeled, cored, and cubed

14 oz (400 g) can crushed tomatoes

1 tablespoon curry powder

1 teaspoon cumin

½ teaspoon paprika

½ teaspoon cinnamon

½ teaspoon turmeric

Pinch dried oregano

Pinch red pepper flakes

½ cup (100 g) red lentils

3 cups (700 ml) chicken or

   vegetable stock

1 cup (250 ml) unsweetened coconut milk

Salt and freshly ground black pepper, to taste

Small bunch scallions, finely chopped

1 cup (150 g) roasted cashews

Heat the butter in a large soup pot over medium-high heat. Add the chopped onion and sauté for 2-3 minutes, stirring occasionally. Add the carrots and cook for another 5 minutes, then add the garlic, ginger, apples, and tomatoes. Stir well and sauté for 5 minutes.

Stir in all the spices. Add the lentils and stock. Mix well and bring to a simmer. Simmer over medium heat for 30 minutes, until the vegetables and lentils are tender.

To purée the soup, fill a blender or food processor no more than halfway. Start on low speed, keeping your hand on top in case the lid pops off from the rising steam. Increase the speed to high and blend until smooth, about 1 minute. You might need to do this in batches.

Return to a clean pot set over low heat. Add the coconut milk, mix well, and taste for seasoning, adding salt and pepper, if necessary.

Ladle into soup bowls. Garnish with the scallions and roasted cashews and serve hot.

Lentil

Paula Wolfert

Lentil and Swiss Chard Soup

SERVES 4–5

---

1 cup (200 g) brown lentils

1 onion, chopped

2 tablespoons extra virgin olive oil

2 small garlic cloves, crushed

2 lb (1 kg) Swiss chard leaves,
  finely shredded

½ cup (15 g) chopped cilantro

Salt, to taste

Freshly ground black pepper

Pinch cayenne pepper

Juice of 1–2 lemons

Thin lemon slices and cilantro
  leaves, to garnish

Rinse and pick over the lentils. Place in a large cooking pot and cover with 6 cups (1.5 l) water. Bring to a boil. Lower the heat and simmer, covered, for about 40 minutes.

About 5 minutes before the lentils are done, wilt the onion in the oil in a large soup pot over medium heat, about 5 minutes.

Stir in the garlic, chard, cilantro, lentils, and all of the cooking liquid. Season with salt, black pepper, and cayenne. Bring to a boil, lower the heat, and simmer, covered, for 15 minutes. Stir in the lemon juice.

Garnish with the lemon slices and cilantro. Serve hot, cold, or at room temperature.

"*Soup for Syria* is a touching visual account of one's experience through the hardship of war. May this book bring a light of hope to everyone's heart and body and may peace be found very soon."

—Paula Wolfert

Lentil

Martyna Monaco

Lentil, Barley, and Potato Soup

SERVES 4

---

2 tablespoons extra virgin olive oil

1 small onion, chopped

1 cup (200 g) pearl barley

1 lb (450 g) potatoes, cubed

¾ cup (150 g) brown lentils

10 fresh basil leaves

Salt, to taste

4¼ cups (1 l) vegetable stock

1 cup (250 ml) yogurt

Pinch paprika

Heat the oil in a large soup pot over medium heat. Add the onion and cook, stirring, for 2-3 minutes.

Rinse the barley in cold water and drain. Add to the pot and sauté for 5 minutes, stirring continuously.

Add the potatoes, lentils, basil leaves, and salt. Stir well to coat with oil.

Add the vegetable stock and bring to a boil. Reduce the heat, cover the pot, and simmer for 30-40 minutes, or until the potatoes and barley are tender. You can add more water if the mixture becomes too thick.

Remove from the heat, stir in the yogurt, and cook for 10 minutes on low heat.

Ladle the soup into warm bowls. Garnish each serving with a sprinkle of paprika.

Lentil

Joe Barza

Lentil Soup with Milk

SERVES 4-6

---

1 tablespoon (15 g) butter

1 large onion, chopped

3–4 medium carrots, peeled and chopped

2 celery stalks, chopped

1 leek, trimmed and chopped

3 potatoes, peeled and cubed

2¼ cups (450 g) red lentils

6 cups (1.5 l) chicken or
   vegetable stock

2 cups (475 ml) milk

1 tablespoon extra virgin olive oil

2 slices rustic bread, cubed

Salt and freshly ground black pepper, to taste

Pinch dried thyme

Pinch cinnamon

2–3 lemons, sliced

Heat the butter in a large soup pot over medium-high heat. Add the chopped onion and sauté for 2-3 minutes, stirring occasionally. Add the carrots, celery, leek, and potatoes and cook for another 1–2 minutes, then add the lentils. Stir well.

Add the stock and milk, stir well, and bring to a simmer. Cook, partially covered, over medium heat until the vegetables and lentils are soft.

Heat the oil in frying pan and lightly fry the bread cubes. Set aside.

Purée the soup, in batches if necessary, using a food processor or blender.

Return to a clean pot set over low heat. Add salt and pepper to taste and simmer gently to heat through.

Ladle into soup bowls. Garnish with the croutons and sprinkle with the thyme and cinnamon. Serve hot, with lemon wedges on the side.

"I have participated in *Soup for Syria* with a love and passion for my cuisine and a desire to be a part of this humanitarian effort. I believe that each one of us should help in any way we can."

—Joe Barza

Lentil

Jill Boutros

Red Lentil Soup with Mint and Lemon

SERVES 4

_____

2 tablespoons extra virgin olive oil

   (or substitute butter)

1 medium onion, chopped

2 small garlic cloves, chopped

Salt, to taste

½ teaspoon Aleppo pepper or paprika,

   plus more for serving

1 medium tomato, chopped

1 tablespoon tomato paste

1 teaspoon dried mint

   (plus more for serving)

1 cup (200 g) red lentils

¼ cup (40 g) coarse bulgar (*burghul*)

4¼ cups (1 l) chicken or

vegetable stock

Juice of 1 lemon

_____

Heat the oil in a large soup pot over medium heat and sauté the onions until soft.

Add the garlic and sauté an additional minute. Season with salt and the Aleppo pepper or paprika. Stir in the tomato, tomato paste, and mint and continue to cook for another 2 minutes.

Stir in the lentils and bulgar, then cover with the stock and 2 cups (475 ml) water. Bring to a boil, lower the heat, and simmer, partially covered, for 1 hour, stirring occasionally.

Sprinkle each serving with a little dried mint and Aleppo pepper, along with a squeeze of fresh lemon juice.

"*Soup for Syria* is an excellent example of collaboration for a worthy cause. As I write, the snow continues to fall here in the mountains overlooking Beirut. I know very well that many refugee families are suffering through the storm, struggling to keep their accommodations warm and their stomachs full. Who wouldn't want to help?"

—Jill Boutros

Lentil

Aglaia Kremezi

Greek Easter Lamb Soup

SERVES 6-8

Head, neck, intestines, and liver of a young
   lamb or 3 lb (2.5 kg) lamb breast on the bone

2 large onions, halved

Salt and pepper, to taste

½ cup (120 ml) extra virgin olive oil

1 bunch scallions, finely chopped

1 small hot chili pepper, finely chopped
   (or substitute dried chili powder to taste)

1 large bunch fresh dill, chopped

2 eggs

Juice of 1 lemon, or more to taste

"This is a wonderful project, a
book that is not just beautiful
and useful, but in addition it
has such an important purpose!
I am happy to be part of it.
I hope it will find its way to
kitchens all over the world, and
so help feed people in need."

—Aglaia Kremezi

Thoroughly wash the lamb head and neck or lamb breast and place in a large stock pot with the onions. Cover with cold water. Season with plenty of salt, and simmer for about an hour, skimming the surface to remove the accumulated froth.

If using, cut the intestines into several pieces, slice them open, and wash thoroughly under running water. In a separate pan, bring some salted water to a boil, and add the intestines. Blanch for 2 minutes, then remove with a slotted spoon and discard the water. Chop the intestines finely (you don't need more than 1 cup of chopped intestines).

When the meat falls easily off the bone, remove the head and neck or breast from the pot. Using a sharp knife cut open the head and separate the meat from the bones. Remove the meat from the rest of the bones and cut into small pieces. Strain the stock and discard the onions. Set the stock aside to cool, then refrigerate it to make it easier to skim off the congealed fat. (Preparations up to this point may be done a day ahead.)

If using, wash the liver well and cut it into small cubes. In a deep skillet, heat the olive oil and sauté the liver, scallions, and chili. Add the meat and intestines, if using, together with the dill, setting some dill aside to garnish. Stir a few times with a wooden spoon. Transfer to a large pot and add the skimmed stock plus an equal amount of water, and bring to a boil. Reduce the heat and simmer for 15 minutes. Taste and season with salt and pepper, if needed.

Beat the eggs in a large bowl with 2 tablespoons water and the juice of 1 lemon. Slowly add cupfuls of the hot soup to the bowl, whisking continuously. When the egg mixture is very hot, return it slowly to the pot over very low heat, stirring well to prevent curdling. Taste, adding more lemon juice if needed. Sprinkle with remaining dill and serve.

Sally Butcher

Iranian Pomegranate Soup (Ash-e-Anar)

SERVES 4

---

3 medium onions

A little oil or ghee

1 teaspoon ground turmeric

½ teaspoon ground cinnamon

1 cup (200 g) split peas

10½ cups (2.5 l) good stock
  (good water would do)

1 lb (500 g) ground lamb

Salt and pepper, to taste

½ bunch each parsley and cilantro,
  washed and chopped

Handful of fresh mint, washed and chopped

1 bunch scallions, washed and chopped

1 cup (175 g) *kritheraki* (orzo) or
  short-grain rice

2 tablespoons sugar

1 cup (250 ml) pomegranate syrup

Fried onions and mint, or pomegranate seeds,
  to garnish (optional)

Meat

Peel and chop two of the onions, and fry them in a little oil in a large pot. Add the turmeric and the cinnamon, followed by the split peas, and then add the stock. Bring to a boil and simmer for about 10 minutes.

Meanwhile, grate the third onion into the ground lamb, add a little salt and pepper, and knead together.

Next, add the chopped herbs and the kritheraki or rice to the soup, and then, once it comes to a boil again, the sugar and pomegranate syrup.

Shape the meat mixture into the babiest of meatballs and plop them in as well. Now let the whole thing bubble very gently for half an hour.

This *ash* is nice garnished with crispy fried onion and mint, or if they are in season, you could strew a few plump pomegranate seeds across the top.

"In Farsi, the word for chef is *ash-paz*— someone who is capable of making *ash*, or herb soup. The *ash* dishes of Iran are held very dearly, and the act of making them is often regarded as an act of love or dedication. I would like to think that as you make this recipe you will remember those who are in exile from Syria, who have no kitchen or soup pot or indeed anyone for whom or with whom to make soup."

—Sally Butcher

Mark Bittman

Korean-Style Beef or Pork Soup with Rice

SERVES 4

---

3 tablespoons vegetable oil

1 lb (450 g) boneless beef chuck or pork
    shoulder, cut into ½ inch (1 cm) chunks

Salt

3 garlic cloves

8 cups (2 l) beef or chicken stock or water

1 cup (185 g) long-grain rice

2 tablespoons sesame seeds

1 teaspoon red chili flakes, plus more for serving

4 scallions

6 celery stalks, plus any leaves

1 tablespoon sesame oil, plus more for serving

3 tablespoons soy sauce, plus more for serving

1 tablespoon rice vinegar

Put 1 tablespoon vegetable oil in a large pot over high heat. When the oil is nearly smoking, add the beef or pork, sprinkle with salt, and cook, stirring once or twice, until it browns in places, 3–5 minutes.

Peel and mince the garlic cloves. When the beef is browned, stir in the garlic and cook for 30 seconds. Add the stock or water, rice, and another pinch of salt. Bring back to a boil and cook (still boiling) until the rice is just shy of tender, 10–15 minutes.

Put the sesame seeds and 1 teaspoon red chili flakes (more or less) in a medium skillet over medium-low heat. Cook, shaking the pan occasionally, until lightly toasted and fragrant, 3–5 minutes.

Trim and chop the scallions, seperating the white and green parts. Chop the celery stalks and any leaves.

When the sesame seeds and red chili flakes are lightly toasted and fragrant, remove the skillet from the heat and stir in 1 tablespoon sesame oil, 2 tablespoons vegetable oil, 3 tablespoons soy sauce, and the rice vinegar.

When the rice is just tender, stir in the celery leaves and the white parts of the scallions. Cook until the rice is fully cooked (it's ok if it's soft) and the celery is crisp-tender, 2 or 3 minutes.

Divide the soup among 4 bowls; drizzle with the sesame-chili oil, garnish with the green scallion parts, and serve, passing more soy sauce, sesame oil, and red chili flakes at the table if you like.

Meat

Helena Zakharia

Middle Eastern Meatball Soup with Vegetables

SERVES 6-8

---

2 cups (350 g) dried chickpeas, soaked overnight

6 cups (1.5 l) beef stock

1 cup (150 g) fine bulgar (*burghul*)

¾ lb (300 g) ground beef

Salt and freshly ground black pepper,
    to taste

3 onions, finely chopped

3 tablespoons vegetable oil

2 tablespoons dried mint

2 tablespoons tomato paste

1 garlic clove, finely chopped

Juice of 1–2 lemons

3 small zucchinis, peeled, seeds removed,
    sliced into crecents

Cook the chickpeas in the beef broth until tender, about 1 hour. (You can use a pressure cooker to save time.)

To make the meatballs: Wash and drain the bulgar. Add the beef, salt and pepper, and one of the chopped onions to the bowl of a blender or food processor, and pulse to a paste. With moistened hands, shape the paste into meatballs the size of marbles.

Heat half of the oil in a large pan and brown the meatballs. Set aside.

Sauté the remaining chopped onion in the rest of the vegetable oil with a sprinkle of salt, until soft and slightly browned. Add the mint, tomato paste, garlic, lemon juice, and pepper. Stir well, and cook for 2 minutes. Set aside.

Spoon the sautéd onion mixture into the cooked chickpeas. Add the zucchini and meatballs. Simmer slowly until the meat is fully cooked and the vegetables are tender, about 15-20 minutes.

Ladle into soup bowls and serve hot.

Nur Ilkin and Sheilah Kaufman

Turkish Black-Eyed Pea Soup with Lamb and Noodles

SERVES 6

---

2 tablespoons (30 g) butter

10 oz (300 g) boneless leg of lamb,
    cut into ½ inch (1 cm) cubes

1 large onion, finely chopped

Sea salt and freshly ground pepper,
    to taste

1 tablespoon tomato paste

5 cups (1.2 l) hot chicken stock

1 cup (200 g) dried black-eyed peas, soaked in
    cold water for 3–4 hours and drained

½ cup (100 g) angel hair pasta broken into
    ½ inch (1 cm) pieces

Dash of cinnamon

Heat the butter in a 3 quart (3 l) pot over medium heat. Add the lamb cubes and sauté until the color changes, 3–4 minutes.

Reduce the heat to medium-low, cover, and cook for about 10 minutes. The lamb should begin to release its juices. Add the onion, mix well, and cook for 3–4 minutes. Season with plenty of salt and pepper, and stir in the tomato paste. Mix well.

Add hot chicken stock and bring to a boil. Reduce the heat to simmer, cover, and cook for 7–8 minutes. Add the peas and continue to cook, covered, for 25–30 minutes. Check to make sure the peas are cooked, then add the pasta pieces. Mix well and continue to cook, covered, for another 7–8 minutes.

Remove the pot from the heat and add the cinnamon to the soup, mixing it in well. Let the pot stand, covered, for 30 minutes so the flavors blend, then serve.

Meat

Patrick Herbeaux

Melon Gazpacho (chilled)

SERVES 4

_____

1 lb (450 g) cantaloupe, peeled,
    seeds removed, and cubed

Juice of 2 lemons

2 tablespoons extra virgin olive oil

Salt and freshly ground black pepper,
    to taste

½ red bell pepper, finely chopped

½ yellow bell pepper, finely chopped

1 small zucchini, finely chopped

Pinch cayenne or paprika

_____

Combine the melon, lemon juice, and oil in a blender or food processor. Blend until smooth.

Add salt and pepper to taste. Chill in the refrigerator for at least 30 minutes before serving.

Ladle into bowls and garnish with chopped bell pepper and zucchini. Sprinkle lightly with cayenne or paprika. Serve cold.

Candice Lorfing

Cream of Mushroom Soup

SERVES 4

_____

3 tablespoons (40 g) butter

1½ lb (700 g) mushrooms, wiped and sliced

1 onion, finely chopped

1 shallot, finely chopped

1 tablespoon flour

6 cups (1.5 l) chicken or
    vegetable stock

½ cup (120 ml) cream,
    plus ¼ cup (60 ml) to garnish

2 tablespoons fresh parsley,
    plus more to garnish

Juice of 1 lemon (optional)

Salt and freshly ground black pepper,
    to taste

_____

Heat half of the butter in a frying pan over medium-high heat. Add the mushrooms and sauté for 5-7 minutes, stirring occasionally. Set aside.

Heat the other half of the butter in a soup pot. Add the onion and shallot and sauté for 2-3 minutes, until they become translucent. Add the flour and cook, stirring, for an additional 2 minutes.

Add the stock and stir very well to break up any lumps of flour. Bring to a boil.

Set aside a quarter of the mushrooms. Stir the rest into the stock. Lower the heat and simmer for 20 minutes, stirring occasionally.

Purée the soup to a creamy consistency in a blender or food processor. You may need to do this in batches.

Return to a clean pot set over low heat. Add the cream, reserved mushrooms, and parsley and stir well. Add lemon juice, if desired, and salt and pepper to taste.

Ladle into soup bowls and garnish each with a tablespoon of cream and some fresh parsley.

Mushroom

"Knowing that all proceeds from the book will go to food relief programs for Syrian refugees, I wanted to contribute what little I could in order to help fulfill this mission. I truly hope we can all make a difference."

—Candice Lorfing

Troth Wells

Thai Coconut Soup with Mushrooms

SERVES 4

Oil, for sautéing

2 scallions or small shallots, very finely sliced

1 cup (125 g) mushrooms, very thinly sliced (Crimini are fine, but you may prefer to use shiitake or other East Asian mushrooms)

1 stick lemon grass

Zest and juice of 1 lime

3–4 makrut lime leaves (sometimes known as kaffir lime leaves)

½ inch piece galangal or ginger, finely sliced

1 bird's eye or other red chili, deseeded and chopped (or leave intact for less heat)

1¾ cups (400 ml) coconut milk

Salt, to taste

1 tablespoon chopped cilantro

In a large pan, heat a little oil and sauté the scallions or shallots. Add the mushrooms and cook them until they soften.

Next, add the lemon grass, lime zest, makrut lime leaves, galangal or ginger, and chili. Stir and cook to blend the flavors.

Now pour in the coconut milk and 1 cup (250 ml) water and stir well. Bring the soup to a simmer and cook for 10 minutes. Add the lime juice and salt, taste and adjust the flavors, and cook for a further 10 minutes.

Remove from the heat and serve immediately, garnished with the cilantro.

"Soup is a communal, sharing food par excellence—food to bring us together wherever we are, and thereby also to bring our thoughts to people who are going through hard times, such as the Syrian refugees and others in the world. Good luck with the project."

—Troth Wells

Mushroom

Rosina Jerkezian

Okra Soup

SERVES 4

———————

2 tablespoons extra virgin olive oil

1 medium onion, chopped

4 small garlic cloves, chopped

1 lb (450 g) okra

2 medium tomatoes, peeled and chopped

Juice of 1 lemon

1 tablespoon tomato paste

Salt, to taste

Small bunch cilantro, finely chopped

———————

Heat the oil in heavy soup pot over medium-high heat and sauté the onion for 1 minute. Add the garlic and stir. Add the okra, tomatoes, and lemon juice.

Dilute the tomato paste in 3 cups (750 ml) water and add to the pot. Season with salt, to taste.

Bring slowly to a boil. Reduce heat to low, cover, and simmer for 20 minutes.

Ladle soup into warm bowls and sprinkle with cilantro just before serving.

Okra

"I'm delighted that my simple soup recipe may touch the lives of the needy and improve their lives."

—Rosina Jerkezian

Chérine Yazbeck

Onion Soup

SERVES 4

––––––––––––

¼ cup (60 ml) extra virgin olive oil

2 lb (1 kg) onion, sliced

1 teaspoon sugar

6 cups (1.5 l) chicken stock

1 cup (250 ml) white wine

1 bay leaf

Pinch dried thyme

Salt and freshly ground black pepper,
   to taste

½ French baguette, sliced into thick pieces

2 cups (200 g) grated Comté
   or Gruyère cheese

––––––––––––

Preheat the broiler to 400°F (200°C).

Heat the oil in a heavy soup pot over medium heat and sauté the onions, stirring, until soft and golden brown, about 10 minutes. Add the sugar after about 1 minute to help the onions caramelize.

Add the stock, wine, bay leaf, and thyme. Bring slowly to a boil. Reduce heat to low, cover, and simmer for 30 minutes. Season with salt and pepper. Discard the bay leaf.

Toast the bread slices in the oven until golden brown, about 3 minutes.

Ladle the soup into heatsafe bowls. Lay the bread on top and sprinkle with cheese. Put under the broiler for 10 minutes at 400°F (200°C), until the cheese is melted and slightly browned.

Serve immediately.

"Destruction, broken dreams, and exile have so far been the outcome of this ongoing war, causing a huge number of Syrians to flee their smashed hometowns in search of a temporary safe shelter... I feel privileged to share one soup recipe and draw more attention to their desperate situation."

—Chérine Yazbeck

Onion

Carolyn Kumpe

Creamy Apple Parsnip Soup

SERVES 6

---

2 tablespoons safflower, sunflower,
   or vegetable oil

2 tablespoons unsalted butter

3 medium leeks or 2 large sweet onions,
   trimmed and chopped

Salt and freshly ground black pepper, to taste

1 tablespoon honey

1 bay leaf

1 sprig fresh rosemary, thyme, or sage

6 cups (1.5 l) chicken stock

1 lb (450 g) parsnips, peeled and sliced

2 large potatoes, peeled and cubed

2 sweet-tart apples, such as Granny Smith
   or Fuji, peeled, cored, and cubed

1 tablespoon apple cider vinegar

¼ teaspoon ground cinnamon

¼ teaspoon freshly grated nutmeg,
   plus more to garnish

¼ cup (60 ml) hard cider or apple juice

½ cup (150 ml) heavy cream

Minced chives, chervil, or scallions, bacon bits,
   sour cream or crème fraiche, grated nutmeg,
   or chopped parsley, to garnish (optional)

Heat the oil and butter in a large soup pot on medium-low heat until the butter is melted. Add the leeks or onions with a pinch of salt. Sauté on low until the leeks or onions are soft, about 8 minutes. Add the honey, bay leaf, and herb sprig. Cook until fragrant, about 1 minute.

Pour in the stock. Add the parsnips, potatoes, and apples. Cover the pan, bring to a simmer, and simmer for 30 minutes or until the fruits and vegetables are tender. Remove and discard the bay leaf and herb sprig. Allow the soup to cool.

Purée the cooled soup with a stick blender, food processor, or blender. Return to the saucepan. Stir in the vinegar, cinnamon, nutmeg, and cider or juice. Cook on low heat for 15 minutes.

Remove from the heat. Stir in the cream and season with salt and pepper. Return the pot to low heat, warming it gently, but do not allow the soup to boil.

Ladle into soup bowls. Sprinkle with grated nutmeg and garnish as desired.

"A simple, pure act of sharing a recipe has turned into an international collaboration of world-renowned chefs. I am honored to take part and hope that we can fill the empty bowls of the many Syrian refugees."

—Carolyn Kumpe

Caline Chaya

Pea Soup
with Mint

SERVES 4

――――――――――――

2 tablespoons extra virgin olive oil

4 shallots, sliced

½ lb (200 g) potatoes, peeled and cubed

2 cups (475 ml) chicken or
   vegetable stock

1 lb (450 g) frozen peas

½ cup (10 g) mint leaves, chopped

½ cup (15 g) arugula, chopped

Salt and freshly ground black pepper,
   to taste

Croutons, to garnish

――――――――――――

Heat the olive oil in a medium soup pot and sauté shallots until translucent. Add the potatoes and stock and bring to a boil. Lower the heat to simmer and cook until the potatoes are tender.

Add the frozen peas and continue to cook for about 3 minutes.

Add the mint and arugula and cook for an additional 5 minutes.

To purée the soup, fill a blender or food processor no more than halfway. Start on low speed, keeping your hand on top in case the lid pops off from the rising steam. Increase the speed to high and blend until smooth, about 1 minute. You might need to do this in batches.

Return to a clean pot set over low heat to heat through. Season with salt and pepper to taste.

Serve warm, topped with croutons.

Pea

"My contribution is simply a way to do my part. *Soup for Syria* will help reach so many people. I wish I could do more."

—Caline Chaya

Cristina Ghafari

Split Pea Soup

SERVES 6

_____

6 cups (1.5 l) vegetable stock

1 cup (250 ml) water

2 medium onions, finely chopped

2 large carrots, peeled and chopped

1 medium potato, peeled and cubed

3 small garlic cloves, finely chopped

2½ cups (500 g) dried yellow split peas

Salt, to taste

2 bunches parsley, finely chopped

½ tablespoon cumin

Croutons, to garnish

_____

Place the stock, water, onions, carrots, potato, and garlic in a large soup pot over high heat. Bring the mixture to a boil.

Add the dried yellow split peas. Turn down the heat and simmer for 30 minutes or until the vegetables are tender and the peas are very soft.

Add salt and the parsley.

Using a stick blender, potato masher, or the back of a metal spoon, mash the peas until the soup is thick and the peas have broken down, adding more water if necessary. Add the cumin and more salt to taste.

Serve hot, garnished with croutons.

Fernando Gomez

Red Pepper Soup

SERVES 4

_____

4 large red bell peppers

3 tablespoons (40 g) butter

1 medium yellow onion, chopped

1 large potato, peeled and diced

3 small garlic cloves, chopped

4¼ cups (1 l) chicken or
   vegetable stock

¼ cup (60 ml) cream or milk

Cayenne pepper, to taste

Salt and freshly ground black pepper,
   to taste

_____

Roast the peppers under the broiler or over an open flame until blackened on all sides (you can also do this on the grill). Seal the blackened peppers in a plastic bag and set aside to steam for 10 minutes, or until the skins feel like they can easily be slipped off. Remove the peppers from the bag, peel off the blackened skins, and remove the seeds. Roughly chop the peppers.

Heat the butter in a large soup pot over medium-high heat. Add the chopped onion and sauté for 2-3 minutes, stirring occasionally. Add the potatoes and cook for another 1–2 minutes, then add the garlic and roasted peppers. Stir well and cook for 2 minutes.

Add the stock, stir well, and bring to a simmer. Simmer over medium heat until the potatoes are soft.

Purée the soup in a blender or food processor until smooth.

Return to a clean pot over low heat. Add cream, stir well, and taste for seasoning. Add cayenne pepper, salt, and black pepper to your liking. Serve hot.

"We can make soup with ingredients from all over the world, so why not peace?"

—Fernando Gomez

Martyna Monaco

Potato and Onion Soup with Sage

SERVES 4

———————————

1 tablespoon (15 g) butter

1 onion, chopped

1 sprig fresh sage

1 lb (450 g) potatoes, peeled and chopped

4¼ cups (1 l) vegetable stock

1 cup (250 ml) milk

Pinch cayenne pepper

Salt and freshly ground black pepper, to taste

———————————

Heat the butter in a large soup pot over medium-high heat. Add the chopped onion and the sage and sauté for 2-3 minutes, stirring occasionally. Add the potatoes and cook for another minute.

Add the stock, stir well, and bring to a simmer. Cook over medium heat until the potatoes are soft, about 30-35 minutes.

To purée the soup, fill a blender or food processor no more than halfway. Start on low speed, keeping your hand on top in case the lid pops off from the rising steam. Increase the speed to high and blend until smooth, about 1 minute. You might need to do this in batches.

Return to a clean pot set over low heat. Add the milk, stir well, and taste for seasoning. Add cayenne pepper, salt, and black pepper as desired.

Potato

Helena Zakharia

Creamy Pumpkin Soup

SERVES 4

———————

2 lb (1 kg) pumpkin or squash, peeled,
    deseeded, and cut into chunks
6 cups (1.5 l) chicken or
    vegetable stock
1 onion, finely chopped
1 garlic clove, chopped
½ teaspoon dried thyme
5 black peppercorns
Salt, to taste
½ cup (120 ml) cream or 1 cup (250 ml) milk
Croutons, to garnish

———————

Place all ingredients except the cream or milk and the croutons in a large soup pot. Bring to a boil, lower the heat, and simmer for 40 minutes.

To purée the soup, fill a blender or food processor no more than halfway. Start on low speed, keeping your hand on top in case the lid pops off from the rising steam. Increase the speed to high and blend until smooth, about 1 minute. You might need to do this in batches.

Return to a clean pot set over low heat. Add the cream or milk and stir well until heated through.

Serve hot, garnished with croutons.

Paola Skaff Alford

Roasted Pumpkin Soup with Cardamom

SERVES 6-8

6½ lb (3 kg) pumpkin

3 tablespoons vegetable oil

2 medium onions, chopped

2 leeks, trimmed and chopped

1 teaspoon sugar

1 tablespoon (15 g) butter

1 teaspoon ground cardamom

Pinch of nutmeg

8½ cups (2 l) vegetable stock

1 cup (250 ml) cream

Salt and freshly ground black pepper,
     to taste

Croutons, to garnish (optional)

Preheat the oven to 350°F (180 °C). Line a baking sheet with parchment paper.

Halve the pumpkin and remove the seeds, scraping the inside clean. Place it upside down on the lined baking sheet. Roast for about 90 minutes, or until tender (check by poking it with a fork). When tender, scoop out the pumpkin flesh and discard the shell. Coarsely chop the flesh and set aside.

Heat the oil in a large soup pot over medium-high heat. Add the chopped onion and leeks. Sauté for 2-3 minutes, stirring occasionally. Add the sugar and butter. Cook for 20 minutes, stirring frequently, until caramelized, then stir in the pumpkin.

Add the spices and stock. Stir well and bring to a simmer. Cook over medium heat until the pumpkin flesh is soft and breaking down.

Purée the soup using a stick blender, food processor, or blender.

Return the puréed soup to a clean pot set over low heat and gently stir in the cream. Add salt and pepper to taste and serve hot, garnished with croutons, if desired.

Pumpkin

"If each one of us decided to commit to one positive action every day, the world would be a better place. War fuels war, love spreads love. My decision to participate in this unique book project is to spread love, compassion, tolerance through mindful action as opposed to mindless reaction. Let's make soup, not war!"

—Paola Skaff Alford

Troth Wells

South American Pumpkin Soup (Sopa de Calabaza)

SERVES 4

---

1 tablespoon margarine

1 onion, sliced

1 lb (450 g) pumpkin, calabash, or butternut
squash, cut into 1 inch (3 cm) cubes

2 garlic cloves, chopped

1 fresh chili, deseeded and finely chopped

1 bay leaf

2 cups (475 ml) tomato juice

¾ cup (200 ml) stock

A little milk (optional)

Salt and pepper, to taste

1 tablespoon chopped parsley, to garnish

First, melt the margarine in a large saucepan and cook the onion until it begins to soften. Now add the pumpkin, garlic, chili, and bay leaf.

Pour in the tomato juice and stock next and bring to a boil. Allow to simmer, stirring from time to time, for 20 minutes or until the pumpkin has softened.

Transfer the soup to a blender or food processor, and blend until smooth, adding a little milk, if desired, for a thinner consistency.

Return to the pan, season with salt and pepper, and heat through before serving, with the parsley sprinkled on top.

Wendy Rahamut

Caribbean Fish Soup

SERVES 6-8

2–4 lb (1–2 kg) whole fish, cleaned, filleted,

and sliced (reserve the head for the stock)

1 large Habanero pepper, deseeded and chopped

2 garlic cloves, minced

1 tablespoon olive oil

2 tablespoons vegetable oil

1 medium onion, chopped

2 large carrots, peeled and sliced

1 potato, peeled and cut into large dice

1½ lb (700 g) mixed root vegetables (yucca, sweet

potato, African yam), peeled and cubed

4 green bananas, peeled and thickly sliced

2 tomatoes, chopped

Salt and pepper, to taste

1 tablespoon (15 g) butter, to serve

FISH HEAD STOCK

½ bunch fresh French thyme

6 whole black peppercorns

4 whole allspice berries

4 garlic cloves, chopped

1 Habanero pepper, deseeded and chopped

1 tablespoon minced chives

2 tablespoons minced cilantro

2 tablespoons fresh lime juice

Salt, to taste

Prepare the fish: Place the fish pieces in a shallow glass dish and toss with the hot pepper, garlic, 1 teaspoon salt, and olive oil. Refrigerate for 1 hour.

Prepare the fish head stock: Place the washed fish head in a medium stockpot with 7 cups (1.6 l) water, thyme, peppercorns, allspice, garlic, hot pepper, chives, cilantro, lime juice, and salt, to taste. Bring the mixture to a boil, then reduce the heat to a simmer, cover, and simmer for 1 hour.

Prepare the vegetables: Heat the vegetable oil in a large, heavy saucepan or Dutch oven and sauté the onion, carrots, and potato for 3–4 minutes.

Strain the cooked fish head stock into the pot containing the sautéed vegetables. Bring the mixture to a boil, reduce the heat to a simmer, cover, and simmer for 30 minutes. Add the chopped root vegetables and the green bananas.

Now, add the chopped tomatoes and the marinated fish pieces and cook slowly for an additional 15–20 minutes, until the fish is cooked and tender. Add salt and pepper to taste and the butter, stir gently, and serve hot.

"The nation of Trinidad and Tobago has a diverse culture with a common thread, feeding as many as we can from one pot. Caribbean Fish Soup (fresh fish, root vegetables, herbs, and fiery peppers) is nourishing, satisfying, and sustaining, the perfect meal to feed masses. I hope this cookbook brings awareness to the plight of refugees. It may not happen overnight, but efforts such as this can ease hunger and diminish suffering."

—Wendy Rahamut

Cristina Ghafari

Fish Soup

SERVES 4-6

---

1 large onion, thinly sliced

3 medium potatoes, cubed

1 rasher of bacon, sliced (optional)

4 small garlic cloves, crushed

2 parsley sprigs

1 tablespoon whole peppercorns

2 bay leaves

1 tablespoon sea salt

1 teaspoon paprika

¼ cup (60 ml) dry white wine (optional)

1 lb (450 g) firm white fish,
   cut into large chunks

Juice of ½ lemon

1 tablespoon extra virgin olive oil

½ teaspoon red pepper flakes

Layer the onion and potato slices in a soup pot with the bacon, if using. Add 3 garlic cloves and the parsley, peppercorns, bay leaves, salt, paprika, and wine. Add enough water to just cover the vegetables and bring to a boil. Lower the heat to simmer and cook until the potatoes are tender, about 15 minutes.

Lay the fish pieces on top of the vegetables, making sure they are just covered in the liquid (add more water if necessary) and simmer for 5–10 more minutes, without stirring, until the fish is cooked through. Remove from the heat.

Make a spicy sauce to garnish the soup: Place two cups of the vegetables and soup stock into a blender or food processor, making sure there are plenty of potatoes. Add the lemon juice, olive oil, red pepper flakes, and the remaining garlic clove. Purée to a thick, creamy consistency.

Serve the soup warm, topped with a dollop of the spicy sauce.

"At a loss for some way to help, on a cold day in December 2013, I began cooking and distributing soup to poor, homeless, and displaced people of my city. I contributed this recipe to *Soup for Syria* because, nutritious and filling, it is one I have made often. I hope it warms your heart as it has for so many."

—Cristina Ghafari

Claude Shehadi

Red Lentil Seafood Soup

SERVES 6-8

---

1 lb (450 g) mussels

¼ cup (60 ml) extra virgin olive oil,
     or more if needed

3 shallots, finely chopped

Scant ½ cup (100 ml) dry white wine

2 small garlic cloves, chopped

2 celery stalks, finely chopped

1 large carrot, finely chopped

2¼ cups (250 g) red lentils (or use brown)

1 tablespoon tomato paste

1 pinch saffron, soaked in 1 tablespoon water

1 teaspoon hot paprika

½ teaspoon black pepper

2–3 bay leaves

3 sprigs lemon thyme

1 lb (450 g) whole sea bass, deboned

½ fennel bulb, finely chopped

Coarse sea salt, to taste

½ lb (250 g) shell-on uncooked shrimp

Chopped parsley, to garnish (optional)

Wash the mussels, discarding any open ones, and trim the beards. Set aside, submerged in cold water.

Heat 1–2 tablespoons olive oil in a large, deep pot over medium heat. Sauté half of the shallots until soft. Add the mussels and toss for a couple of minutes before adding the wine. Bring to a boil and leave to cook for 2 minutes. Reduce the heat and simmer for 15 minutes. By then all the shells should have opened. Discard any unopened shells. Remove the flesh from the open mussels, reserving several in their shells for the garnish. Reserve the cooking liquid for later use.

Preheat the oven to 350°F (180°C).

In a large soup pot, sauté the rest of the shallots in 1–2 tablespoons olive oil until soft. Add the garlic and cook for a further 2 minutes before adding the celery and carrot. Sauté for a few minutes with the lid on to soften the vegetables.

Add the lentils, tomato paste, spices, and 6 cups (1.5 l) water to the vegetables and gently bring to a boil. Tie the thyme sprigs together with a string and add them to the pot. Simmer on medium to low heat for 20 minutes, stirring from time to time.

While the lentils are cooking, place the sea bass in a roasting pan. Fill the cavity with the fennel. Sprinkle with coarse salt and brush with olive oil. Bake for 20 minutes or until cooked. When cooked, remove the skin and set aside.

Just before serving, add the shelled mussels with their cooking liquid to the soup and bring back to a simmer. Add the raw shrimp and allow them to cook for 2 to 3 minutes, until they turn pink. Finally, flake the fish and gently mix it into the soup. Remove the bay leaves and thyme sprigs.

Serve hot, garnished with a sprinkle of parsley and the reserved mussels.

Seafood

Greg Malouf

Moroccan Lentil and Chickpea Soup with Cumin-Fried Whitebait

SERVES 6

¼ cup (60 ml) extra virgin olive oil

1 medium yellow onion, diced

2 small garlic cloves, crushed

½ cup (100 g) brown lentils

½ cup (75 g) dried chickpeas,
    soaked overnight and drained

10½ cups (2.5 l) vegetable stock

14 oz (400 g) can crushed tomatoes

¼ teaspoon ground cinnamon

¼ teaspoon ground ginger

1 pinch ground saffron (about 10 threads,
    lightly toasted and crushed)

Zest and juice of 1 lemon

¼ cup (60 ml) dry sherry

1 tablespoon chopped parsley

1 tablespoon chopped cilantro

1 tablespoon chopped celery leaves

CUMIN-FRIED WHITEBAIT

½ lb (200 g) whitebait

1½ tablespoons cumin seeds, toasted and ground

1 teaspoon ground ginger

½ teaspoon white pepper

1½ cups (200 g) all-purpose flour

3 cups (700 ml) canola oil, for frying

Heat the olive oil in a large pot and gently sweat the onions and garlic until they soften.

Add the lentils, chickpeas, and 8½ cups (2 l) stock. Simmer for 1 hour or until the lentils and chickpeas are soft and beginning to break down.

Use a stick blender on low speed to lightly crush the mixture, but make sure not to create a smooth purée. Add the tomatoes and spices. Bring to a boil and finish off with the lemon juice and zest, sherry, and the fresh herbs. Adjust the consistency with additional stock, if necessary, before removing from the heat.

Wash the whitebait thoroughly and dry on paper towels. Sift the cumin, ginger, and white pepper together with the flour. Heat the oil to 400°F (200°C) in a deep frying pan or deep-fryer. Dust the whitebait with the seasoned flour.

Deep-fry the whitebait in 2–3 batches: Lower the fish gently into the oil and cook for 2–3 minutes, or until golden brown. (They should set into their new shape in the hot oil.) Remove the fish with a slotted spoon or, if using a deep-fryer, lift the basket out of the oil, and transfer the fish to paper towels to drain.

Serve the fried whitebait piled on top of the soup.

Helena Zakharia

Seafood Soup

SERVES 6-8

---

2 tablespoons extra virgin olive oil

2 onions, chopped

4 small garlic cloves, chopped

2 tablespoons tomato paste

2½ cups (600 ml) white wine

28 oz (800 g) can crushed tomatoes

½ teaspoon turmeric

3 bay leaves

2 teaspoons sugar

Salt, to taste

1½ lb (700g) shell-on king (or other
     large) crab legs, cut into large chunks

2 lb (1 kg) firm fish filets, sliced

1 lb (450 g) uncooked shrimp

½ lb (250 g) scallops (optional)

½ lb (250 g) clean squid, cut into
     ½ inch (1 cm) rings

Heat the olive oil in a large cooking pot over medium heat. Add the onions and garlic and cook until the onions are soft.

Add the tomato paste, wine, tomatoes, turmeric, bay leaves, sugar, 1 cup (250 ml) water, and salt, to taste. Bring to a boil, then reduce the heat and simmer for 10 minutes.

Add the crab legs and fish to the mixture. Return to a boil, then simmer for 5 minutes.

Gently stir in the shrimp, scallops, and squid. Return to a boil, reduce the heat, and simmer for an additional 10 minutes, or until the seafood is cooked.

Serve warm.

Seafood

Garrett Melkonian

Spicy Clam Soup with Basturma

SERVES 4-6

3–4 tomatoes, peeled and diced

2 garlic cloves, minced

2–4 tablespoons red pepper paste

Small bunch cilantro, finely chopped,
    plus more to garnish

½ teaspoon cayenne pepper

2 teaspoons cumin

3 tablespoons (45 ml) lemon juice

¼ cup (60 ml) extra virgin olive oil

2 lb (1 kg) manila clams, rinsed and drained

3 cups (700 ml) chicken stock

3½ oz (100 g) basturma (Turkish air-dried
    cured beef, or substitute pastrami), diced

3 tablespoons (45 g) unsalted butter

Grilled or toasted bread, to serve

In a large bowl, combine the tomatoes, garlic, pepper paste, cilantro, cayenne, cumin, lemon juice, and olive oil. Mix thoroughly with a spoon or spatula (do not use a whisk).

Heat a large stockpot over medium-high heat, add the tomato mixture, and cook until the mixture becomes fragrant and tomatoes begin to break down, about 1 minute.

Add the clams, stock, and basturma and bring to boil over high heat. Reduce the heat to simmer, cover, and cook, shaking the pot occasionally, just until all of the clams have opened. Using a slotted spoon, transfer the clams to serving bowls, leaving the broth in the pot.

Add the butter to the broth and check for seasoning. The basturma and the clams carry a good deal of salinity, and the soup will probably not need salt.

Ladle the broth over the clams, garnish each bowl with a handful of cilantro leaves, and serve with thick slices of grilled bread.

"Everyday images of war torn communities, once beautiful and thriving, flood our hearts and fill our souls with grief and the ever-growing need to help those affected by conflict. The *Soup for Syria* project is a message of hope and a giant step towards the light."

—Garrett Melkonian

Marie Carmen Fallaha

Spinach Soup

SERVES 4

————————————

2 tablespoons vegetable oil

1 large onion, chopped

1 small potato, chopped

2 lb (1 kg) spinach, chopped

4¼ cups (1 l) chicken or
    vegetable stock

1 cup (250 ml) cream, plus
    ¼ cup (60 ml) more, to garnish

Salt and freshly ground black pepper,
    to taste

Pomegranate seeds, to garnish

————————————

Heat the oil in a soup pot over medium-high heat. Add the onion and sauté for 2-3 minutes, stirring occasionally. Add the potato and cook for another 1-2 minutes, then add the spinach. Stir well, and cook for 2 minutes.

Add the stock, stir well, and bring to a simmer. Cook over medium heat until the potato pieces are soft.

Purée the soup using a food processor or blender. Start on low speed, keeping your hand on top in case the lid pops off from the rising steam. Increase the speed and blend until smooth. You might need to do this in batches.

Return to a clean pot set over low heat. Add the cream, stir well, and taste. Add salt and pepper as desired. Cook for a further 10 minutes to heat through, without letting it boil.

Serve warm in soup bowls, each garnished with 1 tablespoon of cream and a few pomegranate seeds.

"I decided to participate in this wonderful book after seeing through Barbara's eyes the conditions experienced in the camp. Each of us should help any cause related to the pain of the human race regardless of color or religion."

—Marie Carmen Fallaha

Spinach

Joumana Accad

Carrot
and Sweet
Potato Soup

SERVES 4-6

_____

2 tablespoons (30 g) butter

1 lb (450 g) onions, chopped

1 lb (450 g) sweet potato,
    peeled and cubed

1 lb (450 g) carrots, peeled and chopped

1 tablespoon ground cumin

4¼ cups (1 l) chicken or
    vegetable stock

½ cup (120 ml) cream

Salt and freshly ground black pepper,
    to taste

Pinch red pepper flakes, to garnish (optional)

_____

Heat the butter in a large soup pot over medium-high heat. Add the onion and sauté for 2-3 minutes, stirring occasionally. Add the sweet potatoes and carrots. Cook for another 1–2 minutes, then add the cumin. Stir well and cook for 2 minutes.

Add the stock, stir, and bring to a simmer. Cook over medium heat until the sweet potato is tender, about 30 minutes.

To purée the soup, fill a blender or food processor no more than halfway. Start on low speed, keeping your hand on top in case the lid pops off from the rising steam. Increase the speed to high and blend until smooth, about 1 minute. You might need to do this in batches.

Return to a clean pot set over low heat. Add the cream, stir well, and taste, adding salt and pepper to your liking. Garnish with red pepper flakes, if desired.

Serve warm.

Sweet Potato

"I was touched to the core by the anguished circumstances and plight of the Syrian refugees in Lebanon. I wanted to lessen their terrible burden in some way, yet felt overwhelmed and helpless. I am so grateful for _Soup for Syria._ May our minute contribution help alleviate their sufferings."

—Joumana Accad

Oumayma Nadar

Spicy Sweet Potato Soup

SERVES 4-6

─────────────

½ cup (125 g) plain yogurt

1 teaspoon lime zest

1 tablespoon extra virgin olive oil

1 onion, chopped

2 small garlic cloves, chopped

2 large sweet potatoes, peeled and cubed

4¼ cups (1 l) vegetable stock

½ teaspoon ground cumin

¼ teaspoon crushed red pepper flakes

2 tablespoons grated fresh ginger

¼ cup (50 g) smooth peanut butter
    (homemade is best)

Juice of 1 lime

Salt, to taste

1 large tomato, seeded and diced

2 tablespoons chopped cilantro

─────────────

Mix the yogurt and lime zest in a small bowl. Set aside in the refrigerator to allow the flavors to blend.

Heat the olive oil in a large pot over medium heat. Add the onion and garlic, and sauté until softened, about 5 minutes. Add the sweet potato and vegetable stock. Season with cumin, red pepper flakes, and ginger. Bring to a boil. Reduce the heat to low, cover, and simmer for 15 minutes, until the sweet potato is tender.

To purée the soup, fill a blender or food processor no more than halfway. Start on low speed, keeping your hand on top in case the lid pops off from the rising steam. Increase the speed to high and blend until smooth, about 1 minute. You might need to do this in batches.

Return the soup to the pan over low heat and whisk in the peanut butter. Stir in the lime juice and salt.

Ladle into warm bowls, topping each with a spoonful of the reserved yogurt, a few pieces of chopped tomato, and a sprinkle of cilantro.

"My participation in *Soup for Syria* was a minor contribution to a major humanitarian need. Benevolence has no color, creed, or borders."

—Oumayma Nadar

Tammy Mattar

Sweet Potato and Feta Cheese Soup

SERVES 4-6

_____

¼ cup (60 ml) plus 2 tablespoons

    extra virgin olive oil

2 tablespoons dried wild thyme (*zaatar*)

1 tablespoon (15 g) butter

1 medium onion, chopped

1 large carrot, peeled and chopped

1 leek, trimmed and chopped

5 medium sweet potatoes, peeled and cubed

2 cups (475 ml) chicken or

    vegetable stock

1 bay leaf

Salt, to taste

¼ cup (35 g) crumbled feta cheese

_____

Combine ¼ cup (60 ml) olive oil with the thyme in a small pot. Cook over medium heat until hot, but be very careful not to burn the thyme. Set aside to cool and infuse.

In a large soup pot, heat the butter and the remaining olive oil over medium-high heat. When the butter has melted, add the onion, carrot, and leek. Sauté until the onions have softened, about 5 minutes.

Add the sweet potatoes and sauté for another minute.

Add 6 cups (1.5 l) water, the stock, bay leaf, and salt. Bring to a boil. Once the soup begins to boil, lower to a simmer, and cook for 30 minutes, or until the sweet potato is completely cooked. Remove bay leaf.

To purée the soup, fill a blender or food processor no more than halfway. Start on low speed, keeping your hand on top in case the lid pops off from the rising steam. Increase the speed to high and blend until smooth, about 1 minute. You might need to do this in batches. Check the seasoning and add salt, if needed, keeping in mind that the feta is salty.

Ladle the soup into bowls. Crumble some feta over each bowl, and drizzle with some of the thyme-infused (*zaatar*) oil.

Sweet Potato

Reem Azoury

Summertime Red Gazpacho (chilled)

SERVES 6-8

———————————

5½ lb (2.5 kg) ripe tomatoes, chopped

2 lb (1 kg) baby cucumbers, chopped

2 small garlic cloves, crushed

¼ cup (60 ml) sherry vinegar

Juice of 1 lemon

12 basil leaves, plus more to garnish

½ cup (120 ml) extra virgin olive oil

Salt, to taste

Freshly ground black pepper

———————————

Put the tomatoes, cucumbers, and garlic in a food processor or blender and pulse several times to coarsely chop.

Add the vinegar, lemon juice, and basil. Blend until smooth. Slowly pour in the olive oil while the machine is running.

Season with salt and pepper. If the soup is too thick, add water until it is your preferred texture.

Pour the soup through a medium-hole strainer into a pitcher and refrigerate for at least 1 hour before serving.

Serve cold in glasses, garnished with a few basil leaves.

"Soup is like the light at the end of the tunnel; it whispers to your soul that in the end all will be okay."

—Reem Azoury

Tomato

Helena Zakharia

Roasted Tomato Soup

SERVES 4

---

12 medium tomatoes, quartered

2 small garlic cloves, crushed

1 large onion, quartered

¼ cup (60 ml) extra virgin olive oil

3 sprigs thyme (or substitute
    ½ teaspoon dried oregano)

1 tablespoon sugar

½ bunch basil leaves, plus more to garnish

4¼ cups (1 l) chicken or
    vegetable stock

Salt and freshly ground black pepper,
    to taste

½ cup (120 ml) cream

Sundried tomatoes in oil, chopped

Preheat oven to 450°F (200°C).

Arrange the tomatoes, garlic, onion, olive oil, thyme, sugar, and basil leaves in a roasting pan. Mix well. Roast in the oven until cooked, about 30 minutes. Remove and discard the thyme.

Purée the tomato mixture in a food processor or blender. Add chicken or vegetable stock and process again until smooth. Add salt and black pepper.

Return to a clean pot set over low heat. Heat through, add the cream, stir well, and taste for seasoning.

Ladle into soup bowls and garnish with basil leaves and sundried tomatoes.

Tomato

Martyna Monaco

Tomato
Basil Soup
with Bread

SERVES 4-6

————————————

Scant ½ cup (100 ml) extra virgin olive oil

5 thick slices day-old rustic bread

1 teaspoon salt

Pinch oregano

3 small garlic cloves, thinly sliced

1 onion, finely chopped

10 basil leaves

2 lb (1 kg) large ripe tomatoes, sliced

4¼ cups (1 l) vegetable stock

————————————

Place all the ingredients in a large soup pot over medium heat in the following order: olive oil, bread, salt, oregano, garlic, onion, basil, tomatoes, and vegetable stock.

Bring to a boil. Lower the heat, cover the pot, and simmer gently for 1 hour, stirring occasionally. The soup is ready when the bread breaks down and the soup is thick.

Ladle into bowls and serve hot.

Tomato

Ana Sortun

White Turnip and Hazelnut Soup

SERVES 4

———————

4 cups (500 g) peeled and cubed sweet white
   turnip (Hakurei or Macomber)

1 small fennel bulb, outer leaves and core
   removed, roughly chopped

1 small leek (white part only), roughly chopped
   and cleaned

2 garlic cloves, peeled and sliced

2 tablespoons olive oil

1–2 teaspoons salt

1 teaspoon ground black pepper

½ cup (60 g) hazelnuts, lightly toasted and skins
   removed, plus about 12 reserved for garnish

5 cups (1.25 l) rich chicken broth

2 teaspoons honey

½ cup (120 ml) almond milk or milk

2 tablespoons finely minced chives or scallions

2 tablespoons brown butter, for drizzling
   over the top (optional)

Sumac, for sprinkling over the top (optional)

———————

Make sure you select a white, creamy, sweet turnip for this soup. I like to use the Hakurei turnip or Macomber turnip for this recipe, but cauliflower is also a great substitute.

Place the vegetables in a large soup pot with the garlic, olive oil, salt, and pepper and stir to coat them. Cook them gently over medium heat until they begin to soften but don't brown.

Stir in ½ cup (60 g) of the hazelnuts and add the broth. Simmer the soup until the vegetables are completely soft and tender, about 20 mintues. Allow the soup to cool.

In a blender or food processor, blend the soup with the honey and milk. Taste and adjust the seasoning.

Reheat gently and ladle the soup into bowls. Garnish each bowl with some minced chives or scallions, a teaspoon of brown butter, a sprinkle of sumac, and some slightly crushed hazelnuts.

"There is hope that this marvelous collection of soup recipes from chefs all over the world will remind us of those in Syria who have lost their homes and so much more. Let us all make soup to create some relief and provide more outreach to those that are in need."

— Ana Sortun

Iman Sabbagh

Chicken Soup
with Freekeh

SERVES 4-6

———————————

1 whole free-range chicken

   (about 3½ lb/1.5 kg)

2 onions, 1 peeled and 1 finely chopped

2 carrots, peeled

1 small cinnamon stick

3 whole allspice berries

1 sprig parsley

1 bay leaf

Salt, to taste

1 cup (200 g) roasted green wheat (*freekeh*),

   whole grain or cracked grain

———————————

Place the chicken in a large pot with water to cover. Bring to a boil over medium-high heat, using a mesh skimmer to remove any foam that rises to the surface. Once the liquid reaches a boil, reduce the heat, and add the whole onion, carrots, cinnamon, allspice, parsley, bay leaf, and salt. Simmer gently until chicken is cooked, about 60–90 minutes. Continue to skim the foam occasionally.

Lift the chicken from the broth and set aside until cool enough to handle. Remove and discard the bone, cartilage, and skin. Separate the chicken meat into smaller pieces and set aside.

Add the chopped onion and freekeh to the broth, bring to a boil, lower the heat, and simmer, covered, until soft (10–15 minutes for cracked wheat, 45–60 minutes if using whole grain). You may need to add more water, depending on the consistency you prefer.

Add the chicken pieces as soon as the freekeh becomes tender. Adjust the seasoning.

Serve steaming hot on a cold winter's day.

Wheat

"My contribution to *Soup for Syria* is a small gesture to help the Syrian refugee community overcome the struggles of daily life."

—Iman Sabbagh

Diala Kourie

Kishk Soup

SERVES 4-6

¼ cup (60 ml) extra virgin olive oil

1 small onion, chopped

1 garlic clove, chopped

7 oz (200 g) ground beef or lamb (not too lean)
 or Lebanese preserved meat (*awarma*)

Salt and freshly ground black pepper, to taste

1 medium potato, cubed

1 cup (150 g) *kishk* (fermented dried
 yogurt with bulgar; look for it in Middle
 Eastern grocery stores)

Heat the oil in a large soup pot over medium-high heat. Add the onion and sauté for 2-3 minutes, stirring occasionally. Add the garlic. Stir in the ground meat or *awarma*. Season with plenty of salt and pepper.

Add the potato and leave to cook over low heat for 5 minutes.

Pour in the dried *kishk* and 4¼ cups (1 l) water and simmer, stirring constantly, until the mixture thickens and the potatoes are tender, about 10 minutes. It should have the consistency of loose porridge (add more water if needed).

Serve warm.

"We all long for the same basic rights and dignity regardless of our race, political, and religious beliefs."

— Diala Kourie

Necibe Dogru

Shepherds' Soup

SERVES 4-6

---

1 cup (150 g) coarse bulgar (*burghul*)

Salt and freshly ground black pepper,
   to taste

1 egg (organic is best)

2 cups (500 g) plain yogurt

Scant ½ cup (100 ml) extra virgin olive oil

1 tablespoon dried mint

Place the *burghul* in a sieve and wash until the water runs clear. Transfer to a medium saucepan.

Add 6 cups (1.5 l) water and salt and pepper. Cover and bring to a boil over high heat. As soon as the water boils, reduce the heat to medium-low. Leave to simmer until all the liquid is absorbed, about 15 minutes. Remove from heat. Let the *burghul* rest, covered, for 5 minutes. Remove the lid and fluff with a fork.

Break the egg into a bowl, add the yogurt, and thoroughly whisk. Pour gently over the cooked *burghul*. Cook on very low heat until the yogurt warms but does not boil.

Combine olive oil and dried mint in a small saucepan. Cook over medium heat until hot, being very careful not to burn the mint. Pour over the cooked *burghul* and mix thoroughly.

Serve immediately.

Yogurt

"Sharing a recipe is a small gesture in the face of the immense distress of the large number of refugees displaced by the war in Syria. I wholeheartedly hope that this cookbook initiative will bring some of them some comfort."

— Necibe Dogru

Rosina Jerkezian

Armenian Zucchini Soup

SERVES 4

_____

½ lb (225 g) beef chuck or other stewing cut,

    cubed and cooked (optional)

2 lb (1 kg) zucchini, chopped

    (or use pumpkin for a variation)

¾ cup (150 g) canned or cooked chickpeas

¼ cup (60 ml) extra virgin olive oil

3 small garlic cloves, crushed

1 teaspoon dried mint

2 tablespoons tomato paste

Juice of 2 lemons

Salt, to taste

_____

Combine the beef and 4¼ cups (1 l) water in a large soup pot. Bring to a boil, lower the heat to simmer, and cook, covered, for about 1 hour or until the meat is tender (skip this step for vegetarian soup). Add the zucchini slices and simmer until tender, then add the chickpeas, and simmer for 5 more minutes.

In a separate saucepan, heat the oil and add the garlic, dried mint, and tomato paste. Stir for about 1 minute, then stir the mixture into the zucchinis.

Add the lemon juice and salt to taste, cover, and simmer for a few minutes to heat through.

Serve hot.

Zucchini

Sana Wakeem Awad

Zucchini Basil Soup

SERVES 4

_____

1 tablespoon butter or vegetable oil

1 large onion, chopped

2–3 small garlic cloves, chopped

6 medium zucchinis, chopped

1 tablespoon all-purpose flour

4¼ cups (1 l) chicken stock

1 small bunch fresh basil leaves

1 small bunch fresh parsley, chopped

½ cup (120 ml) milk or cream (optional)

Salt and freshly ground black pepper. to taste

_____

Heat the butter in a large soup pot over medium-high heat. Add the onion and sauté for 2-3 minutes. stirring occasionally. Add the garlic and cook for another 1–2 minutes. then add the zucchinis. Stir well and cook for 2 minutes.

Dissolve the flour in the chicken stock. Add to the soup pot. stir well. and bring to a simmer. Add the basil. Cook over medium heat for 20 minutes. or until the vegetables are tender. Add the parsley at the very end to add color to the soup.

To purée the soup. fill a blender or food processor no more than halfway. Start on low speed. keeping your hand on top in case the lid pops off from the rising steam. Increase the speed to high and blend until smooth. about 1 minute. You might need to do this in batches.

Return to a clean pot set over low heat. Add the milk or cream. if using. Stir well and taste. adding salt and pepper as desired.

Zucchini

Patrick Herbeaux

Zucchini, Pear, and Cilantro Soup

SERVES 4

---

2 tablespoons extra virgin olive oil

1 onion, chopped

1 leek, trimmed and chopped

1 garlic clove, crushed

2 zucchinis, chopped

2 pears, peeled and chopped

½ cup (100 g) short-grain rice

6 cups (1.5 l) vegetable stock

1 small bunch cilantro

Handful arugula leaves

Salt and freshly ground
    black pepper, to taste

Heat the olive oil in a large soup pot over medium-high heat. Add the chopped onion and leek and sauté for 2-3 minutes, stirring occasionally. Add the garlic and cook for another 1–2 minutes, then add the zucchini, pears, and rice and stir well.

Add the stock, stir well, and bring to a simmer. Cook, partially covered, over medium heat until the rice is cooked, 15–20 minutes.

Add the cilantro and arugula and cook for 5 minutes.

To purée the soup, fill a blender or food processor no more than halfway. Start on low speed, keeping your hand on top in case the lid pops off from the rising steam. Increase the speed to high and blend until smooth, about 1 minute. You might need to do this in batches.

Return to a clean pot set over low heat to heat through. Season with salt and black pepper and serve hot.

Zucchini

Contributors

Joumana Accad is a Lebanese-American pastry chef, blogger, and cookbook author. She is the founder of TasteofBeirut.com and author of *A Taste of Beirut* (HCI, Inc).

Paola Skaff Alford recently moved to Bali from Beirut. She is an artist, cook, yogi, and a mother of two. Mixing colors is her passion, from fabrics to painting to ingredients in the kitchen.

Sana Wakeem Awad is a chef, gardener, and food writer. She lives in a farmhouse in Jordan, grows organic herbs and vegetables, and produces homemade jams. She trained at the Glion Institute Switzerland (2006) and studied pastry and bakery with Puratos Company in Belgium (2007).

Reem E. Azoury was owner and chef of Figs Fine Foods in Washington, DC for seven years. She now lives in Beirut, where she creates original menus and new food concepts for Meat the Fish.

Joe Barza is a Lebanese Master Chef with over 22 years of experience in the culinary field. He has earned numerous awards in international culinary forums, where he has represented his country with pride and honor. A popular television personality, Joe co-hosted season one of the television program 'Master Chef' in the Middle East. He is Founder and Chef Consultant of Joe Barza Culinary Consultancy, a member of the Academie Culinaire de France, the German Chefs Association, and the organizing committee of the Lebanese Salon Culinaire HORECA.

Mark Bittman is one of America's best-known and most widely respected food writers. He covers food policy, cooking, and eating as an opinion columnist and blogger for the *New York Times*, where he is also the *New York Times Magazine*'s lead food writer. He produced 'The Minimalist' column for 13 years, now a show on the Cooking Channel; he is also a regular on the *Today Show* and he has authored more than a dozen cookbooks, including *How to Cook Everything*, *How to Cook Everything Vegetarian* (both also available as apps), and *Food Matters*. Learn more at markbittman.com.

Chris Borunda was born and raised in Los Angeles, California. After completing a bachelor's degree from Tohoku University in Sendai, Japan, he attended the Culinary Institute of America in Hyde Park, New York. He apprenticed in Germany and France before returning to New York, where he is Chef de Cuisine at Montmatre restaurant.

Anthony Bourdain is chef, author, and raconteur best known for traveling the globe on his stomach, on his TV show *Anthony Bourdain: Parts Unknown*, a travel docu-series for CNN, which won two Emmy Awards in 2013 and a Peabody Award and Emmy Award in 2014. He is the author of the bestselling *Kitchen Confidential: Adventures in the Culinary Underbelly*, the travel journal *A Cook's Tour*, the memoir *Medium Raw*, 3 crime novels, a cookbook, a biography of Typhoid Mary, the bestselling graphic novel *Get JIRO!*, and numerous others.

Jill Boutros is a winery and restaurant owner. She lives in the mountains overlooking Beirut and the Mediterranean Sea. In addition to creating world-class wines from her organic vineyards, she is a cooking and baking enthusiast who has fallen under the spell of Lebanon's incredibly tasty, fresh, and seasonal produce.

Sally Butcher is the fiery-haired proprietress of Persepolis, the notable Persian food store and cafe in London, which she runs with her husband, Jamshid. She is also a prolific cookbook author and blogger. Her first book, *Persia in Peckham*, was selected Cookery Book of the Year by the *Times* of London and was short-listed for the 2008 André Simon Award. *The New Middle Eastern Vegetarian*, *New Middle Eastern Street Food*, and *Salmagundi: A Celebration of Salads from around the World*, all published by Interlink, have also received critical acclaim.

Caline Chaya trained at L'Institut Paul Bocuse. She is Jamie Oliver's Food Revolution Ambassador in Beirut, Lebanon.

Laurie Constantino lives between Anchorage, Alaska, and Limnos, a rural Greek island in the Northern Aegean Sea. In both kitchens, the foods of the Mediterranean play a starring role. She is a cooking teacher and the author of *Tastes like Home: Mediterranean Cooking in Alaska*. She writes about food on www.laurieconstantino.com.

Alexis Couquelet is group executive chef and partner of The Alleyway Group. He has a B.A. in Culinary Arts from the Academy of Culinary Arts in New York, and over 20 years of experience working for prominent restaurants and caterers in Paris, the USA, and Lebanon, alongside some of the most respected names in French gastronomy. He currently lives in Beirut, where he is owner and executive chef of two branches of Couqley restaurants.

Marie Carmen Fallaha is a Mexican-born interior and fashion designer based in Lebanon. She is founder and designer of the brand *Emme*, whose flagship store is in downtown Beirut.

Cristina Ghafari is event planner for Slow Food Beirut. Raised in New York, of Portuguese descent, she now lives with her family in Lebanon. Since December 2013, she has cooked and distributed soup weekly to the homeless and displaced near her home.

Fernando Gomez started cooking for family and friends as a young boy in his native country, Mexico. After attending culinary school, his passion in life became his journey. He is now in Beirut, where he shares his passion for food with his own Mexican twist.

Aziz Hallaj is a consultant on urban planning, development, and local governance. He is a visiting assistant professor at the American University in Beirut. In 2007, he received the Aga Khan Award for Architecture.

Pascale Hares is a graphic designer born, raised, and taught right from wrong in Beirut, Lebanon. She lives in the mountains with her husband, their two boys, and a yellow Labrador, who is fortunately a female. She teaches corporate identity at Alba University and works from home creating logos, identities, illustrations, and recipes for good people. She designed *Soup for Syria*. Learn more at www.pascalehares.com.

Patrick Herbeaux is a medical doctor and the founder and creator of Pailettes et Confitures, a line of gourmet jams and fruit preserves. His passions are traveling and cooking for friends and family.

Jane Hughes is a food writer, production manager, and publisher. She worked with The Vegetarian Society for over 20 years and was formerly the editor of the *Vegetarian* magazine. Her writing has appeared in London's the *Guardian*, BBC *Vegetarian Good Food* magazine, and *Resurgence* magazine, among others. She is author of several books, most recently, *The Adventurous Vegetarian: Around the World in 30 Meals* (The New Internationalist).

Nur Ilkin is a food writer, cooking instructor, and co-author of *A Taste of Turkish Cuisine* and *The Turkish Cookbook* (Interlink). She learned the secrets of Turkish cooking from her grandmother, but it was as a Turkish ambassador's wife that she perfected her culinary skills while entertaining diplomats and dignitaries.

Rosina Jerkezian is a passionate cook and blogger. Her blog showcases a variety of traditional Armenian and Lebanese dishes and promotes healthy, slow cooking.

Aline Kamakian gave up a successful career in insurance to pursue her passion for food. In 2003, along with her cousin **Serge Maacaron**, she opened Mayrig Beirut, a contemporary Armenian restaurant celebrating the often forgotten flavors of ancient Armenia. Since then, Aline has ventured into new concepts, opening The Kitchen, M Catering, Mayrig Jeddah, Batchig by Mayrig, and Mayrig Boulevard Restaurant in Dubai, with a branch soon to open in Riyadh.

Sheilah Kaufman is a food writer, lecturer, cooking instructor, and author of 26 cookbooks, including the bestselling *The Turkish Cookbook* (co-authored with Nur Ilkin). She is a founding charter member of the International Association of Culinary Professionals and has written for numerous publications, including *Vegetarian Times*, the *Washington Post*, the *Tampa Tribune*, and the *Baltimore Sun*.

Beatrice Khater was born in Spain in 1967. She is a family physician and the mother of two girls.

Diala Kourie is a Lebanese-Syrian woman living in Belgium since 1987.

Aglaia Kremezi introduced Greek cooking to an American audience with her Julia Child Award-winning book *The Foods of Greece* and now leads a cook's tour of the entire region with her latest book, *Mediterranean Vegetarian Feasts*. Her blog, *Aglaia's*

Table (http://www.aglaiakremezi.com), chronicles food and life on the Greek island of Kea where she lives and teaches cooking to lucky travelers (www.keartisanal.com).

Carolyn Kumpe worked for more than 20 years in highly acclaimed Northern California restaurant kitchens. She is the chef and owner of Vendage & Company, catering events in the Sierra Nevada Foothills Wine Country. Her recipes have appeared in the *Sacramento Bee*, as well as magazines such as *Southern Living, Country Home, Sunset, Reader's Digest, Taste of Home, Cooking Light, Rachel Ray, Sacramento Magazine*, and more. She is a long-term member of the Slow Food Society and the International Association of Women Chefs.

Candice Lorfing is half Bosnian and half Lebanese. She is a mother of two, an avid cook, a food lover, and an adventurous baker.

Greg Malouf, born in Melbourne, Australia to Lebanese parents, is a Michelin-starred chef widely regarded as the modern Middle Eastern master. He is the co-author, with his former wife Lucy Malouf, of the multi-award-winning cookbooks *Arabesque, Moorish, Saha, Turquoise, Saraban, Malouf: New Middle Eastern Food*, and recently, *New Feast: Modern Middle Eastern Vegetarian*.

Barbara Abdeni Massaad is a food writer, TV host, cookbook author, and a regular contributor to international cooking magazines. She is author of several cookbooks including *Man'oushé: Inside the Lebanese Street Corner Bakery* (also published by Interlink) and *Mouneh: Preserving Foods for the Lebanese Pantry*, which won the the Gourmand Cookbook Award and the International Academy of Gastronomy Award. She is a founding member of Slow Food Beirut and an active participant in the International Slow Food movement. She lives in Beirut with her husband and three children.

Garrett Melkonian is Executive Chef of Mamnoon, a Lebanese restaurant based in Seattle, Washington.

Martyna Monaco was born in Naples, Italy. She has a degree in gastronomic science and currently works for Slow Food Cremonese. Her biggest passion is studying the food heritage of Mediterranean countries.

Oumayma Nadar studied at St. Martin's School of Art and the Byam Shaw School of Painting in London. After a decade in the art world, she opened the House of Chi in 2000, pioneering the provision of traditional meditative and martial arts and healing therapies in Dubai, U.A.E. The Wellness Project is her latest venture.

Yotam Ottolenghi is a cookery writer and chef-patron of the Ottolenghi delis and NOPI restaurant. He writes a weekly column in the *Guardian's Weekend* magazine and has published four bestselling cookbooks: *Plenty* (his collection of vegetarian recipes), *Plenty More*, and, co-authored with Sami Tamimi, *Ottolenghi: The Cookbook* and *Jerusalem*. Yotam has made two 'Mediterranean Feasts' series' for More 4, along with a BB4 documentary, 'Jerusalem on a Plate.' Read more at: http://www.ottolenghi.co.uk.

Veronica Pecorella grew up working in her family's old *osteria* in a small village in Northern Italy. Cooking and sharing food has always been her passion. She works in the agricultural, agro food, and restaurants quality certification sector and is a member of the Advisory Council of the Mediterranean Citizen's Assembly (ACM).

Wendy Rahamut is the author of several Caribbean cookbooks including *Caribbean Flavours, Modern Caribbean Cuisine* (Interlink), and *Curry, Callaloo & Calypso*. She is a freelance food consultant and food stylist and the weekly food writer for the *Trinidad Guardian*. She owns the Wendy Rahamut School of Cooking and has been the host and producer of a long-standing weekly cooking show series titled *Caribbean Flavours* since 1998. She lives in Trinidad.

Claudia Roden was born and brought up in Cairo. Her books include *The Book of Jewish Food*, which won eight international awards, as well as *The New Book of Middle Eastern Food, Arabesque, Coffee: A Connoisseur's Companion, The Food of Italy: Region by Region, Everything Tastes Better Outdoors*, and *Mediterranean Cookery*. In 1989 she won Italy's two most prestigious food prizes, the Premio Orio Vergani and the Premio Maria Luigia, Duchessa di Parma. She has also won six Glenfiddich awards. She now lives in London.

Iman Sabbagh is owner of Tayebat Iman, a small bakery in south Lebanon established in 2000. A pioneer in encouraging and supporting local farmers to grow chemical-free grains, Iman produces healthy, sugar free, conventional confections, whole wheat bread, sweets, and nut butter.

Claude Chahine Shehadi began her career as a filmmaker. She is a self-taught cook and the author of three cookbooks about the Mediterranean kitchen. She is co-founder of The Libaliano Kitchen and teaches workshops on Lebanese cuisine. She lives in Boston, Massachusetts.

Ana Sortun is cited as one of the country's "best creative fusion practitioners." She graduated from La Varenne Ecole de Cuisine in Paris before opening Moncef Medeb's Aigo Bistro in Concord, Massachusetts, in the early 1990s. Following stints at 8 Holyoke and Casablanca in Harvard Square, she opened Oleana in 2001, immediately drawing raves for her Middle Eastern dishes that the *New York Times* described as "rustic-traditional and deeply inventive." After being awarded the "Best Chef: Northeast" honor by the James Beard Foundation in 2005, her bestselling cookbook, *Spice: Flavors of the Eastern Mediterranean*, was published in 2006 and nominated for a James Beard Award in 2007. In 2010, Ana appeared on Season 2 of Bravo's *Top Chef Masters*.

Sami Tamimi is executive head chef across the three Ottolenghi London-based delis. He is in the kitchen every day, creating new dishes and innovative menus as well as developing and nurturing young kitchen talents. Alongside Yotam Ottolenghi, Sami Tamimi is co-author of two bestselling cookbooks: *Ottolenghi: The Cookbook* and *Jerusalem*, which won the James Beard "Best International Cookbook" award and the Observer Food Monthly "Best Cookbook" Award, among others.

Sona Tikidjian is a small-scale producer who sells delicious, homemade, traditional Armenian dishes at farmer's markets throughout Beirut, Lebanon.

Linda Toubia was born in the south of Lebanon and has been cooking for as long as she can remember. She is a mother of five, grandmother of ten, and great-grandmother of two.

Alice Waters is a chef, activist, and proprietor of Chez Panisse Restaurant and Café, and has championed local, sustainable farms for more than four decades. She has been awarded the James Beard Best Chef in America, France's Légion d'Honneur, and the Lifetime Achievement award from *Restaurant Magazine*'s World's 50 Best Restaurants. She is the author of many cookbooks, most recently *40 Years of Chez Panisse*, *In the Green Kitchen*, and *The Art of Simple Food*.

Troth Wells is the acclaimed author of numerous cookbooks including *Small Planet, Small Plates: Earth-Friendly Vegetarian Recipes*, *One World Vegetarian Cookbook*, and *Global Vegetarian Cooking: Quick and Easy Recipes from around the World*, all published by Interlink.

Paula Wolfert is widely acknowledged as one of the premier food writers in America and the "queen of Mediterranean cooking." She writes a regular column in *Food & Wine*, alternating with Jacques Pepin and Marcella Hazan, and she is author of 11 cookbooks, including *The Food of Morocco*, *The Slow Mediterranean Kitchen*, and *The Cooking of Southwest France*. Wolfert's writings have received numerous awards, including the Julia Child Award, the M.F.K. Fisher Award, the James Beard Award, the Cook's Magazine Platinum Plate Award, and the Perigueux Award for Lifetime Achievement. Her articles have appeared in the *New York Times*, *Saveur*, *Fine Cooking*, and *Cook's Illustrated*. In 2008, she was inducted into the Cookbook Hall of Fame by the James Beard Association.

Chérine Yazbeck is an independent photojournalist and head of the Levant Desk at Transterra Media, a Beirut-based press agency. She is the author of numerous books including *A Complete Insiders Guide to Lebanon*, *The Rural Taste of Lebanon*, and *Le Liban Gourmand*.

Acknowledgments

I would like to thank all those who participated in this humanitarian cookbook project and contributed to it directly and indirectly. It is amazing how many of us were involved. I will start with Cristina Ghafari, who gave me the idea to focus on soup. Watching her making her soups every week at the Slow Food Earth market in Hamra to feed the refugees inspired me greatly. Martyna Monaco gracefully offered her time for cooking and many other aspects. My Italian daughter!

Thank you to Slow Food Headquarters in Italy, Suzy Daher, Karma Valluy and her family, and Ursula Valluy for their generous donations, which helped fund this project. Thank you to Lisa Debbane, Maya Nader, Cathy Sultan, Charlotte Hamaoui, Little Helps Association, Catherine Kassouf, Laura Fallaha, and Nathalie and Claude Shehadi for their donations to buy foodstuff and other necessities for the refugees. Great thanks to Zoomaal, the crowd funding platform, for their initial work to raise funds for the project.

Thank you to Rodolphe Ghossoub for introducing me to the people from UNICEF, namely Maria Assi from Beyond, who welcomed me to the refugee camps with open arms. A great appreciation to Turkey Al Ghati and his family: you will always have a special place in my heart.

I would like to thank all the acclaimed and talented chefs who answered my call and contributed to this cookbook: Joumana Accad, Paola Skaff Alford, Sana Wakeem Awad, Reem E. Azoury, Joe Barza, Mark Bittman, Chris Borunda, Anthony Bourdain, Jill Boutros, Sally Butcher, Caline Chaya, Laurie Constantino, Alexis Couquelet, Necibe Dogru, Marie Carmen Fallaha, Cristina Ghafari, Fernando Gomez, Aziz Hallaj, Pascale Hares, Patrick Herbeaux, Jane Hughes, Nur Ilkin, Rosina Jerkezian, Aline Kamakian, Sheilah Kaufman, Beatrice Khater, Diala Kourie, Aglaia Kremezi, Carolyn Kumpe, Candice Lorfing, Serge Maacaron, Zeina El Zein Maktabi, Greg Malouf, Tammy Mattar, Garrett Melkonian, Martyna Monaco, Oumayma Nadar, Yotam Ottolenghi, Veronica Pecorella, Wendy Rahamut, Claudia Roden, Iman Sabbagh, Marina Ana Santos, Claude Chahine Shehadi, Ana Sortun, Sami Tamimi, Sona Tikidjian, Linda Toubia, Alice Waters, Troth Wells, Paula Wolfert, Chérine Yazbeck, and Helena Zakharia.

From the bottom of my heart, I would like to give thanks to friends and colleagues who offered me help, support, and encouragement throughout the process of putting together this book: Diana Aboulhosn, Bashar Alsharani, Amale Bassile, Maroun Chedid, Sandra Dagher, Mona El Dorr, Maria Sevine Fakhoury, Carmen Fallaha, Victoria Frolova, Lina Abdeni Hoffman, Mario Haddad JR, Wassef Haroun, Zeinab Jeambey, Annie Kabakian, Randa Kacha, June Kettaneh, Hanan El Khatib, Lionel Lopez, May Metni, Therese Mourkos, Carole Nader, Nelida Nassar, Tony Rami, Nadime Rawda, Betty Saleh, Alexandra Stratou, Jacqueline Massaad, Vivianne Zakka, and Lorenza Zgheib.

All the recipes in this book were tested by a wonderful group of people who generously gave their time and energy to both cooking and helping me arrange the photo shoots. They include: Martyna Monaco, Chris Borunda, Patrick Herbeaux, Sandra Dagher, Pascale Hares, Cristina Ghafari, Zeinab Jeambey, Brita Rafi, John Mazraani, Chérine Yazbeck, and Maya Zakharia. Thanks also to Helena Zakharia for providing the props.

A special thank you to Pascale Hares for designing the book and donating her time to the project; Karma Valluy for her tips and endless support; and Jill Boutros for editorial help. This book would not have had the impact desired had it not been for the hard work of Michel Moushabeck, publisher of Interlink Publishing. A special thank you to Leyla Moushabeck and the rest of the team at Interlink—Jen Staltare, Pam Fontes-May, John Fiscella, Ann Childs—for patiently going through the whole book and making sure all is perfect.

To my loving husband Serge who never stops encouraging me; to Albert, Maria, and Sarah, my children, who are the light of my life; may our loving family always be ready to help those who are in need.

And finally, I owe a debt of gratitude to all the refugees in the Bekaa Valley who trusted me and collaborated with me in good faith even though they had no idea what I was trying to achieve. I pray that they and their beautiful children will find a way to endure and overcome these harsh times until they are able to get back to their homeland, Syria. I pray for peace and security for all.

Index